This Old Corvette

The Ultimate Tribute to America's Sports Car

With stories, photographs, and artwork from Peter Egan, Mike Antonick, Noland Adams, Zora Arkus-Duntov, Allan Girdler, Lucinda Lewis, Martin Milner, John C. Amgwert, Dave Barnhouse, Vince Crain, James "Kingneon" Guçwa, Kent Bash, Dale Klee, Andrew Morland, Jerry Heasley, and more

Voyageur Press

A TOWN SQUARE BOOK

Edited by Michael Dregni
Designed by JoDee Mittlestadt
Printed in China

03   04   05   06   07   5   4   3   2   1

Library of Congress Cataloging-in-Publication Data

This old Corvette : the ultimate tribute to America's sports car / edited by Michael Dregni.
     p. cm.
"A town square book."
 ISBN 0-89658-622-7 (hardcover)
 1. Corvette automobile. 2. Automobiles—United States.
 I. Dregni, Michael, 1961–
 TL215.C6 T477 2003
 629.222'2—dc21
                              2002014477

Distributed in Canada by Raincoast Books,
9050 Shaughnessy Street, Vancouver, B.C. V6P 6E5

Published by Voyageur Press, Inc.
123 North Second Street, P.O. Box 338
Stillwater, MN 55082 U.S.A.
651-430-2210, fax 651-430-2211
books@voyageurpress.com
www.voyageurpress.com

Educators, fundraisers, premium and gift buyers, publicists, and marketing managers: Looking for creative products and new sales ideas? Voyageur Press books are available at special discounts when purchased in quantities, and special editions can be created to your specifications. For details contact the marketing department at 800-888-9653.

On the frontispiece:
1958 Corvette magazine advertisement. C5 Corvette. (Photograph © Jerry Heasley) Vintage Route 66 postcard.

On the title pages:
Artist Scott Jacobs's painting "Endless Summer." (Artwork © 2002 by Scott Jacobs/Segal Fine Art)

On the acknowledgments page:
1961 Corvette Dealer Promotional Postcard

On the contents page:
Classic Corvette profile. (Photograph © Jerry Heasley)

Acknowledgments

Our thanks to everyone involved with this project, including in alphabetical order: Noland Adams; John C. Amgwert; Bob Antonick; Mike Antonick; Dave Barnhouse; Kent Bash; Thos. L. Bryant at *Road & Track*; Janet Burt; Chaz Cone; Vince Crain; Peter Egan; Allan Girdler; James "Kingneon" Guçwa; Chris Hansen at Hadley Licensing; Jerry Heasley; Bill House; Jerry Irwin; Scott Jacobs; Dale Klee; Lucinda Lewis; Michael McBride; Andrew Morland; Sheila Moss; Floyd M. Orr; Krista Rea at Segal Fine Art; Barbara Spear; Lisa Stanick at Chevrolet Motor Division–GM; Peter Tytla; and John Wakefield.

Contents

This Old Corvette

Most of us who have automobiles in the blood remember the first time we saw a Corvette. Whether it was one of the dazzling 1953s, a stylish split-window 1963 Coupe, or the latest C5, 'Vettes have a way of catching the eye—and often, of changing lives. For most of us, time could be divided into the years before our first Corvette encounter and after. Suddenly, everything in the world looked different.

There's no easy explanation for this, except for the simple fact that Corvettes are not just cars, even to the ordinary Joe or Jill. Corvettes are an American icon revered around the globe. They're a household name, art on wheels, a fantasy in curvaceous fiberglass and chrome, a full-throttled declaration of independence, a poke in the eye to the status quo, an obsession, a religion, a way of life. Martin Milner drove one as Tod Stiles in *Route 66*. Roger Penske raced one, as did Dale Earnhardt. The Beach Boys, Jan and Dean, and Prince all sang rock'n'roll anthems to them. If ever there was a legendary sports car, the Corvette is it.

Many of the stories, tall tales, essays, and reminiscences in this anthology tell of that first Corvette in one way or another. Memories are what this book is all about, and the authors of the pieces collected in this anthology come from a wide range of backgrounds. Several are Corvette "celebrities"; some are respected automotive journalists, authors, and historians; others are regular folk with a story to share about their special Corvette. Selections come from Zora Arkus-Duntov, the godfather of the Corvette, as well as Martin Milner. Among the well-known historians and authors are Peter Egan, Mike Antonick, Noland Adams, Allan Girdler, and John C. Amgwert, and Jerry Heasley. Other authors include Michael McBride, Bill House, Sheila Moss, Chaz Cone, Barbara Spear, John Wakefield, and Floyd M. Orr.

The photography comes from a variety of well-known photographers and archives, including Lucinda Lewis, Jerry Heasley, Andrew Morland, Jerry Irwin, and others.

In addition, there are paintings and art from Dave Barnhouse, Vince Crain, Peter Tytla, James "Kingneon" Guçwa, Kent Bash, Dale Klee, Scott Jacobs, and others.

If you are still in awe of that first Corvette, still driving and tuning Corvettes, or still dreaming of Corvettes, then this book is for you.

Facing page:
A 1966 Corvette convertible tears up the open road. (Photograph © Jerry Heasley)

Inset:
1960s Corvette Hot-Rod Decal

History According to the Chevrolet Corvette

1951: A fan of English sports cars—the Jaguar XK120, in particular—and sports-car racing, General Motors Vice President of Styling Harley Earl begins designing a sports car for GM.

1952: Harley Earl presents his proposal for a two-seater sports car—code-named the "Opel"—to General Motors management. Creation of a sports-car prototype is approved for GM's 1953 traveling auto show, Motorama. After deciding against naming the new sports car the "Corvair," the "Opel EX-122" is christened the "Corvette." The name is suggested by photographer Myron E. Scott of Chevrolet Public Relations because "it began with a 'C,' rolled well off the tongue, and reflected the excitement of a fast World War II warship named the 'Corvette.'"

1953: The prototype Chevrolet Corvette is displayed in January at Motorama in New York's Waldorf-Astoria Hotel. Chevrolet begins Corvette production on a temporary assembly line at Chevrolet Plant Number 35 in Flint, Michigan. On Tuesday, June 30, the first production Corvette, serial number E53F001001, rolls off the assembly line. All 1953 Corvettes were painted Polo White with red interiors and had a sticker price of $3,513. Just 314 Corvettes are built in 1953—although only 183 are sold.

1954: Corvette production moves in December 1953 to a General Motors Assembly Division factory in St. Louis, Missouri. Production of the 1954 Corvette totals 3,640—although 1,076 go unsold.

1955: Zora Arkus-Duntov is made chief engineer in charge of the Corvette. Just 700 1955 Corvettes are built, the lowest annual production number following 1953.

1956: The all-new 1956 Corvette body bows at New York City's Waldorf-Astoria Hotel on January 1 for the 1956 Motorama. Corvette sales reach a record 3,467.

1957: The 1957 Corvette debuts with the miracles of fuel injection and a fully synchronized four-speed manual transmission. Corvette sales almost double to 6,339. Chevrolet begins publishing its *Corvette News* owner's magazine.

1958: Sales of the 1958 Corvette skyrocket to 9,168—and the car turns a profit for Chevrolet for the first time!

1959: Corvette sales climb to 9,670.

1960: The CBS show *Route 66* debuts on October 7 on television screens across the country, featuring Martin Milner, George Maharis, and a 1960 Corvette convertible in search of adventure. Corvette sales finally break the goal of 10,000 annual sales, reaching 10,261.

1961: Production hits 10,939.

1962: Secret production begins on the lightweight Corvette Grand Sport factory racer designed for competition in World Championship races against the might of Enzo Ferrari. Corvette production tops 14,531.

1963: The 1963 Corvette features a new chassis with independent rear suspension and a stunning new body, based on Bill Mitchell's Sting Ray. Sales almost double to 21,513.

1964: Corvette sales continue to climb to 22,229.

1965: Big-block V-8 engines of 396 ci with 425 hp debut in the Corvette as the L78 option. Corvette sales grow to 23,564.

1966: A new 427-ci big-block V-8 is unveiled as a Corvette option. Sales rise to 27,720.

1967: The L88 big-block engine option is quietly announced with its 427-ci engine fathering 500 hp. Corvette sales decline slightly to 22,940.

1968: A new Corvette is introduced, based on the old chassis but with a modern "Coke-bottle-shaped" body and new interior. Sales hit a record 28,566.

1969: The 250,000th Corvette rolls off the production line as Corvette sales top 38,762.

1970: Sales plummet to 17,316—the lowest annual level since 1962.

1971: Corvette sales rebound to 21,801.

1972: Sales increase to 27,004.

1973: Corvette sales hit 30,464. The premiere Corvette Corral show—forerunner to the Bloomington Gold—is held in Bloomington, Illinois.

1974: Corvette sales climb to 37,502.

1975: The 500,000th Corvette drives off the assembly line as sales increase to 38,465.

1976: Sales rocketed to 46,558.

1977: Sales continued to climb to 49,213.

1978: The 1978 Corvette Indianapolis 500 Pace Car leads off the 62nd Indianapolis 500 race. The debut Bloomington Gold Corvette show opens. Sales decline slightly to 46,776.

1979: Sales jump to 53,807.

1980: Sales drop to 40,614.

1981: The last Corvette built in the St. Louis plant rolls off the assembly line as Corvette production is jump-started at a new factory in Bowling Green, Kentucky. Sales total 40,606.

1982: The first Corvettes at Carlisle meet is held. Corvette sales drop to 25,407.

1983: Just 43 1983 Corvettes are built, but they have so many problems that GM halts production.

1984: The largely new 1984 Corvette is launched in March 1983. The extended production run reaches 51,547.

1985: Sales hit 39,729.

1986: A convertible makes a welcomed return to the Corvette lineup for the first time since 1976. The 70th Indianapolis 500 race is led by a 1986 Corvette convertible pace car. Sales total 35,109.

1987: Corvette sales declined to 30,632, which included 10,625 convertibles.

1988: The Corvette celebrated its 35th anniversary with a special-edition model. The National Corvette Museum

Foundation is established but ground breaking in Bowling Green waits until 1990. Production declined again to 22,789.

1989: Sales hits 26,412.

1990: Corvette sales total 23,646.

1991: Sales decline to 20,639

1992: The one-millionth Corvette—a white LT1 convertible with red interior—rolls off the assembly line. The Corvette Americana Hall of Fame opens its doors in Cooperstown, New York. GM executives approve the design of the C5 Corvette—with a planned release date of 1997. Sales rest at 20,479.

1993: The Corvette's 40th anniversary is honored with the Z25 option package. Sales climb slightly to 21,590.

1994: The first 1997 model C5 Alpha test car is built. The new National Corvette Museum opens at the Corvette factory in Bowling Green, Kentucky, with 4,000 Corvettes and 118,000 people visiting. Corvette sales reach 23,330.

1995: A 1995 Corvette paces the 79th Indianapolis 500 race. Corvette sales drop to 20,742.

1996: C4 production ends. Construction of the first C5 model begins on September 3, and the first production 1997 model Corvette is completed on October 1. Sales drop slightly to 21,536.

1997: Chevrolet announces the 1997 Corvette, known as the "C5." Production glitches hold back sales to just 9,752.

1998: The C5 convertible is launched. Corvette sales skyrocket to 31,084.

1999: A hardtop C5 model is announced, the first time that three Corvette models are available. Production soars to 33,270—the highest since 1986.

2000: A 2000 Corvette paces the 24 Heures du Mans. Sales continue to climb to 33,682.

2001: Corvette sales jump to 35,627.

2002: Sales are expected to top 2001 sales.

CHAPTER 1

The Corvette Dream

1957 Corvette Convertible

(Photograph © Jerry Heasley)

Will I Ever Buy a Corvette?

By Michael McBride

The internet has opened up a vast electronic world for people to share their car fascination, something Michael McBride does from his home in Iowa in his e-zine "Common Car" column.

Michael's essays examine the role the common car plays in our everyday lives, from the need for mini-vans for hauling children to our lust for owning a Corvette.

Facing page:

"American Roadway"
Icons of Americana fill artist James "Kingneon" Guçwa's painting of a 1957 Corvette convertible, creating a larger-than-legend image of the classic machine. (Artwork © James "Kingneon" Guçwa)

Inset:
1964 Corvette Sting Ray Brochure

There are more fundamental questions in life than "Will I ever buy a Corvette?" However, many of my car friends and dreamers everywhere have asked or continue to ask this question. After all, today's Corvette is indeed the best of the breed. No less than *AutoWeek* magazine has picked the Corvette over and over in its Top 10 American cars listing. For 2001, *AutoWeek* said the Corvette was number one—the top U.S. auto. Even among world-class cars, like BMW, Porsche, and Acura, the Corvette holds up well.

Yet can the American Supercar be pursued by common buyers? This is a tough call, and maybe my own history can shed some light on this.

When I was in the fifth grade way, way back in 1967–1968, my friend Ronald had an older brother who had just bought a Corvette convertible. I don't recall what engine it had, but the exterior was white. We would often look at it while we were playing. It was a wonderful machine, and we all decided that yes, indeed, we too were all going to buy Corvettes.

When 1972 rolled around, I got my driver's license. Naturally, I couldn't have a Corvette then—I had no money—and thus a 1963 Pontiac Station Wagon was my sports car.

Later, in 1979, I was home from college for the weekend and my old friend Crazy Al the truck driver had just bought a new Corvette. He took me out for a spin, and this was my first actual ride in a Corvette. It was awesome. However, I was just about to graduate from college with no permanent job and a bunch of school loans, so there was no Corvette opportunities there for me.

Still later, in 1985, my old college roommate Mike stopped by to visit us. He had just purchased a C3 Corvette. This was my first chance to actually drive a Corvette. It was better than an MG, but this model was pretty rough. It broke down on us that day, and we had to hustle to find a mechanic late on a Saturday evening to get it back home. As for me, well, we had just bought a house and had a baby, so there were no plans for a Corvette here.

My Corvette dreams really disappeared for the most part. I did enter a few raffle contests and bought a lottery ticket every now and then, but no real serious interest. Still, I never missed the Corvettes on display at the auto show.

Main Street

A customized Corvette shines in the neon lights of main street on a Saturday night. (Photograph © Jerry Irwin)

Then, in October 2000, I assisted the principal at the local high school in the homecoming parade. About six adult men were used as "guards" for a dozen Corvettes. These cars were owned by members of the local Corvette club, who were driving the king and queen candidates in the parade. Who knows what those crazy teenagers might do to these cars—maybe even *touch* them!—so we were tasked to keep an eye on them. They were mostly C4 and C5 cars, and they were indeed wonderful. None of the adults who assisted with the parade had even been close to owning a Corvette despite being a successful, well-educated group. It was amazing to hear other men, all about my age, with similar incomes and families, say the exact same thing: They had always wanted a Corvette, but it never really fit the program.

So I thought about this. When would be a good time for me to buy a Corvette? Well, certainly not now! There is an unstable, war economy. Energy supplies and prices could vary greatly in the next two years. I have two children starting college in the next five years. Then . . . then . . . then . . .

Well, I guess I'll just drop this note off to Chevrolet:

- ◆ I really like the new Corvette Z06
- ◆ Among poor-quality GM products, this is a gem
- ◆ I will speak highly of Corvettes and encourage my friends to buy them
- ◆ I wish you continued success, at least for twenty to thirty more years, so that when I get around to buying a new Corvette you are still there.

Let's hope for the best for both of us. Until then, it's back to the Contours, Tempos, and Rangers.

Wigwam Village

A 1960 Corvette convertible parks alongside its concrete teepee at the famous Wigwam Village motel along Route 66 in Holbrook, Arizona. Built during the 1940s and 1950s, three Wigwam Village motels still stand today. They were designed by architect Frank Redford, who asked that he be paid for his work by the proceeds from the coin-operated radio next to each bed. (Photograph © Lucinda Lewis/All Rights Reserved)

Dreaming Corvettes:
The Tantalizing and Alluring Brochures

When you're dreaming of a Corvette, there is nothing more tantalizing and alluring than paging through a Corvette brochure—except sitting or driving the Corvette of your dreams. Here is a sampling of Corvette brochures from the beginning, chronicling the different eras and styles of Chevrolet's sales literature.

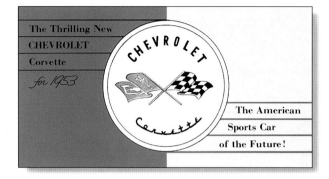

Top:
1953 Corvette Brochure

Above:
1954 Corvette Brochure

CHEVROLET'S
NEW CORVETTE
for 1957

FUN!

1957 Corvette Brochure

1965
CORVETTE
STING RAY

1965 Corvette Brochure

1971 Corvette Brochure

'74 CORVETTE

BUILDING A BETTER WAY TO SEE THE U.S.A. Chevrolet

1974 Corvette Brochure

CORVETTE

1985 Corvette Brochure

2002 Corvette Brochure

The Ego Car

By Sheila Moss

Newspaper humor columnist Sheila Moss has written about subjects as varied as wily Tennessee politicians, the correlation between junk collections and rednecks, and the joys of parenting. Yet her favorite subject is her favorite car, the Corvette.

In this essay, Sheila explains all the myriad reasons why one shouldn't own a Corvette—and just a few good, overriding reasons in favor.

Facing page:
A Sign of Good Taste
Coca-Cola's 1958 advertisement featured two elderly speedsters in their new Corvette at the neighborhood drive-in.

Inset:
1984 Corvette C4 Brochure

have this thing about Corvettes. About six years ago, I bought my first one, a white 1992 model. My first big mistake was the day I let a salesperson talk me into a test drive. From that day on, I just couldn't get that Corvette out of my mind. Being a practical person, I kept trying to justify my need for one in some way. If I could just find one redeeming value to justify it, perhaps I could rationalize it to myself.

Gas mileage? Nope, the big engine was a gas hog and had to have super premium gas.

Comfort? Needed a shoehorn to get in and out of those low bucket seats, and it rode rough, built for performance not luxury.

Space? No room for anything, low overhead, no backseat, and no trunk.

Safety? Don't make me laugh! One of the worse records on the road! Getting insurance is a nightmare! Even with a perfect driving record, my insurance company said they would have to cancel me—just because it was a Corvette.

Economy? Expensive and still just a glorified Chevy.

Nope, there is not one practical thing about a Corvette.

But I wanted it! It was sleek and beautiful and had those cute little headlights that flip up! Yes, I had the fever. I didn't know then what all 'Vette owners know—it's the fever. Corvettes just get in your blood.

So, darn the precautions, full speed ahead. I bought the car and found out about life in the fast lane. I knew I liked it, but what I hadn't realized was how other people would react. It's amazing! Remember when you had a new car, how everyone looked at it, and how it made you feel special to drive it? Well, it's like that every time you drive a 'Vette. People always look and always make comments. They call it the Corvette Mystique. There are clubs just for Corvette owners, magazines with Corvette news and tips. Corvette is the only car with its own museum dedicated just to that car. Antique Corvettes become classic cars worth a fortune. There are shows and runs, a whole culture built around the car. And I just thought I was buying a pretty car!

Then there is driving it! All that power, the way the engine roars, the way it practically leaps out from under you, the way you have to hold back all the time to keep from getting speeding tickets.

Yep, I had a lot of fun with my ego car. Traded it in not long ago with over a hundred thousand miles on the odometer. Never regretted buying it for a minute.

Heck, on a warm summer day with the top off, I could nearly always get at least one marriage proposal yelled at me by a passing motorist. Truck drivers were the worst, of course. They would blow their horns, or make that little sound with their air brakes when I went past. Of course, I knew I was hard to see in that low sports car and tried to stay out of their way as much as possible.

Anyone who ever owned a Corvette even once in their life always wants to talk about it. Funny thing, most of them are not owned by teens either; most are owned by middle-aged people. They always say they had wanted one their whole life. It's a dream car, I guess.

So, that's the story on my ego car, but it isn't over. I traded it for another one! The legend lives! I love it!

"C5"
Home sweet home, complete with a C5 Corvette, as portrayed by artist Kent Bash. (Artwork © Kent Bash)

☆ ☆ ☆

Me and My 'Vette

By Bill House

For some of us, a Corvette is not just transportation but a true time machine linking together our past, present, and future. Bill House's Corvette has been part of his life since 1967. The car, affectionately known as "Gopher," has had three owners, all of whom have remained friends over almost four decades.

ack in the fall of 1962, I was a sophomore in high school sitting in the library. As I was glancing through some car magazines, I saw it! They called it the "Sting Ray." This was the new Corvette, and I couldn't believe my eyes. Nor could I believe it when my homeroom teacher, Mr. Yerkish, drove one to school shortly thereafter. A red, split-window fuelie. I got my first ride in his Corvette when he took me to the optometrist to have my eye glasses repaired so I could play in the JV basketball game that afternoon. I was hooked.

In 1966, Uncle Sam moved me from my hometown of Crafton, a suburb of Pittsburgh, Pennsylvania, to Travis AFB in northern California. I bought a 1964 Malibu SS with a small-block 327 for go power. It wasn't enough. So one of my Air Force buddies, Mike Hayden, helped me put a 396 big-block in the Chevelle. Now, we're talking. About that time, another buddy, Terry McLaren, drove onto base from Alice, Texas, in his 1967 sunfire yellow, black stinger, black interior, black softtop 427/435 Corvette roadster. What a car! And he actually let me take it for a spin.

In the summer of 1969, Terry ordered a new Silver 427/400-horse car from the local Chevy dealer. All of us wanted to buy "Gopher," as the '67 was affectionately called since Terry always used the '67 to "Go for this" and "Go for that." Yet no one could come up with the $2,800 it took to pry the '67 from Terry. Mike Hayden had just come back to Travis after spending thirty days at home in Ohio. After selling everything he owned, and working during his leave, he was happy to hear that "Gopher" was still available. Mike and Terry came to terms and the deal was done.

The '67 was sitting off base at a local body shop for some wheelwell repair. When Mike tried to start her, "Gopher" just coughed. It seems someone had taken her for an unauthorized test drive. Since this car had a five-year, 50,000-mile warranty, the next stop was the local Chevy dealer. After much discussion with the service manager, a new block and intake were supplied and installed by GM under warranty. At the time, "Gopher" had 28,000 miles on the clock, and a lot of those were on trips to and from Texas.

Mike let my wife and I use the '67 to go on a three-day trip to my father-in-law's birthday party from April 14 to 16, 1970, during the same time Apollo 13 was in trouble. Shortly after, in May 1970, Mike's car was stolen and stripped. The body was recovered in August 1970, and most of the interior was recovered in September 1970. Mike actually went with the police and physically removed "Gopher's" parts from several different cars. The door panels to this day have the police markings from when they were recovered. The man who stole the '67 would steal Corvettes and strip them down to a shell. He would then buy the shell at the insurance auction and put the cars back together and sell them. But us poor G.I.'s only had the minimum liability insurance coverage, so there wasn't any auction. The thief was caught when he started selling the individual parts.

At that same time, Mike got his orders to Viet Nam. The car sat in Joe Cruces's body and custom shop in Vacaville, California, for the time Mike was in Nam. Mike would think of ideas while over there and send them home to Joe. Joe worked on Mike's ideas and added a number of his own.

When Mike returned to the States, he decided to finish the project himself as money was a little tight. It took him until the fall of 1977 to finish. During the customizing, a 1968 Buick Riviera grill was molded onto the front of the car to give it the "Mako Shark" look that was so popular at the time. Mike also had the wheelwells radiused and flared. A mild spoiler was added to the rear, and 1967 Mustang taillights replaced the round ones. The hardtop was fitted with a rear window from a 1968 AMX and molded onto the deck lid giving "Gopher" a fastback look. Most of the exterior chrome was removed. The interior was left stock, and when sitting inside the car, you would be hard pressed to know you were inside a custom car. The engine was never located, so Mike bought a 1969 350/350 with a Muncie four-speed to motivate him. After that, he just trailered the car around the western United States to car shows for a number of years.

I had moved away in 1970 and lost track of Mike. Then, in 1984, I moved back to Vacaville. I saw Mike one day in a local store. After talking over old times the conversation got around to "Gopher." Mike said he still had her, so we went over to his house to see her. I told him I would like to have a Corvette myself. After years of talking, in April 1988, Mike finally agreed to sell me the '67. It's a decision he regrets to this day. Every time his son Ryan sees "Gopher," he asks his dad, "Why did you sell?" Mike just gives him a blank stare.

Millenium Yellow

A 2000 C5 Corvette convertible glows in the sunlight in front of an old barn. The Millennium Yellow exterior paint for the year 2000 cost an extra $500 but turned heads on any street anywhere. (Photograph © Jerry Heasley)

As before, small-blocks don't do it for me. I test drove a new ZR1, and I'm sorry but I wasn't impressed. So one of the first things I did was trade the 350 for a 427. Mike Hayden rebuilt the 427 for me. Then he added aluminum heads and a Tri-Power intake.

Next, I repainted the car. I also found a new rear deck lid, a convertible top frame, big-block hood, and other miscellaneous parts. I still have the custom hard-top, so whenever I want a fastback, I put the hardtop back on.

In the meantime, my son decided he wanted a Camaro. We found a damaged 1967 RS that was minus an engine and tranny. So we bought back the 350 that was in "Gopher" and slid it into the Camaro. Now, three years later, my son has a nice driver.

As a repayment for the money I spent on his project, my son decided I needed 17-inch cast "Lotus"

Boyd's wheels on the Corvette—17x8 on front and 17x9½ on the rear. So "Gopher" is now shoed with 275/4OZR on the rear and 235/45ZRs on the front, Goodrich Comp TIAs all around.

About six months ago, I was looking at the guest book from my wedding back in 1969. All of my old buddies that I hadn't seen or heard from in twenty-seven years were in the book. As I came across Terry McLaren's name, I noticed he listed his Texas address instead of the Air Force base address like everyone else. So I thought I would write and see what happens, but since I hadn't seen or heard from Terry since 1970, I was not hopeful.

To my amazement, a week later I received a letter. Terry's mother still lives in that same house, and she said she would give Terry a message. Two weeks later, I got a phone call from him. It seems Terry still has a few

toys in his Texas garage, a 1966 big-block Corvette being one.

One month later, he called again. This time, he was in town. We drove over to my place, got in old "Gopher" and drove across town to Mike Hayden's house. Jerry could not get over the fact that only 40,200 miles registered on the odometer, and he was sitting in the same seats, touching the same door panels, dash pads, steering wheel, and driving over the same streets he had twenty-seven years earlier. After getting Mike out of bed—he works nights—we spent the afternoon talking over old times. I regret I forgot my camera and didn't get any pictures of the three of us with "Gopher."

I have often thought of selling her—I know I have two buyers chomping at the bit, Mike and Terry—but I would have to contend with my family. My son is my biggest contention, and he thinks he will own "Gopher" some day. He just might, but not without a price. I also have two daughters, and when it comes to the 'Vette, all my children think alike. Once a Corvette gets in your blood, especially a big-block mid-year, there is only one cure.

"Field of Vettes"
The true field of dreams for Corvette enthusiasts comes alive in this painting by artist Dale Klee. (Artwork © Dale Klee)

*Well, she's metal-flake blue with a Corvette mill
And they say it looks better when she's standin' still
When I step on the gas she goes wa aa aa
I'll let you look but don't touch my custom machine
—The Beach Boys' "Custom Machine," 1963*

Owning Corvettes:
Operator's and Owner's Manuals

Many people never even bother to read their Corvette's owner's manual, believing they can figure it all out for themselves or preferring to just twist the knobs and push the buttons until they get things right. Whether you read your manual or not, chances are you've held it in your hands feeling immense pride at actually owning your Corvette.

Right:
1953–1954–1955 Corvette Operator's Manual

Bottom:
1956 Corvette Operations Manual

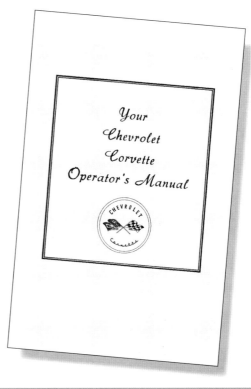

Your Chevrolet Corvette Operator's Manual

1956 OPERATIONS

MANUAL

CORVETTE

owners guide

1963 Corvette Owners Guide

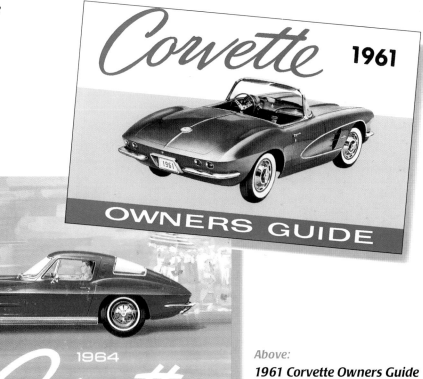

Above:

1961 Corvette Owners Guide

Left:

1964 Corvette Owners Guide

1965 CORVETTE OWNERS GUIDE

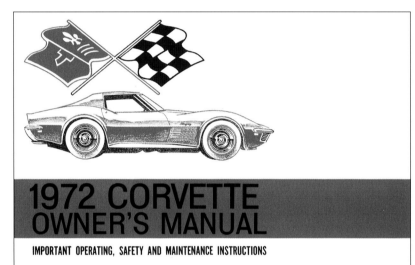

1972 CORVETTE
OWNER'S MANUAL
IMPORTANT OPERATING, SAFETY AND MAINTENANCE INSTRUCTIONS

Top, left:
1965 Corvette Owners Guide

Center, left:
1972 Corvette Owners Manual

Left:
1997 Corvette Owners Manual

966 OWNER'S GUIDE

Above:

1966 Corvette Owners Guide

Right:

1978 Limited Edition Corvette Owners Manual

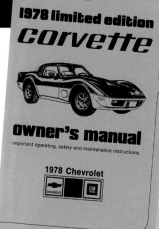

1978 limited edition
Corvette

owner's manual

Important operating, safety and maintenance instructions.

1978 Chevrolet

CHAPTER 2

America's Star-Spangled Sports Car

"Hometown Hero"
The "hometown hero" returns in his Corvette in this painting by Dave Barnhouse.
(Original art by Dave Barnhouse © 2002 Hadley Licensing, Bloomington, MN)

* * *

A Corvette Family History

By Allan Girdler

Allan Girdler's hobbies and career have been intertwined around engines and wheels. Allan is a former editor of *Car Life* and *Cycle World* as well as an executive editor of *Road & Track* magazines. He is also the author of an eclectic blend of books on motoring history, including one of the earliest books on Corvette history, *Automobile Quarterly's Corvette: A Piece of the Action; Impressions of the Marque and the Mystique* as well as his numerous books on motorcycles, such as *Harley-Davidson: The American Motorcycle, Harley Racers, The Harley-Davidson and Indian Wars, Illustrated Harley-Davidson Buyer's Guide, Harley-Davidson XR-750*, and tomes on NASCAR and sports-racing specials.

Allan's own fascination with cars and motorcycles had humble beginnings, as he relates in this essay of Corvettes in the family.

Facing page:

"Welles's Garage"

Photo-montage artist Peter Tytla creates fantastical images of happy car enthusiasts and their world. As Tytla writes about this image: "Ol' Bud Welles is alive, well, and open for business, specializing in machine work, welding, and Corvette parts—and also, occasionally, some fairly fresh gas. Bud will work on just about any Corvette, and will even let you watch. It will 'purr like a kitten' when he's through, and you'll even get your car back fairly quickly."

Inset:

1958 Corvette Brochure

*M*y dad wasn't mechanically inclined. It wasn't a matter of motor skills; he played varsity basketball in college and tennis well into his eighties. But he wasn't handy around the house, didn't fix or tinker, and perhaps because he'd grown up in a time when the family car was the only car in the family, our station wagon was transportation and nothing more.

Then my older brother went away to college.

This was very much another time, as in back then colleges had rules, the students obeyed said rules, and one was no cars for freshmen.

Stranger still, sports cars had become fashionable for those who could afford fashion, and members of the gentry acquired exotics like Jaguars and Porsches and MGs and Lancias and such.

They were stylish and fun, if not always fast. They were also quirky and demanding and tough on the spine and the complexion.

So it happened that when Ford introduced the Thunderbird, a significant share of the drivers of these demanding little charmers traded them in for a car that had style and performance (sorry, but the Corvette of the day offered only dependability) but didn't need to be actually driven, not with automatic and power assists and low-stress V-8.

Thanks to supply and demand, the Ford store's used car lot was fronted by sports cars, at bargain prices. Our hot rod club became a sports car club. My brother sold his channeled '32 Ford three-window coupe and bought an Austin-Healey 100-4, the early model with sidecurtains, no ground clearance, and a windshield that folded down for extra speed.

My dad had noted all this with bemusement. His value system can be deciphered by the fact that he suggested I buy a Willys Jeepster instead of an MG-TC: They both looked funny and old fashioned to his eyes, while the MG had only two seats and the Jeepster could carry three or four pals. (I explained as delicately as I could why I only wanted room for one other person.)

Ferrari Red
Striking a pose that would make a Ferrari green with envy, this Torch Red 2001 C5 Corvette is lowered on all four corners. (Photograph © Jerry Heasley)

Then my brother left for college. He asked dad to run the Healey every week or so, to keep the seals damp, the gas fresh, and the battery charged.

Next thing I knew, there was my brother's car, parked with the top down. Dad got a cap and mom a kerchief, just like the Christmas poem, and they were zooming around town and into the country, not the least deterred by the eccentric SU carburetors, the graunching of the muffler on driveways, or the rain slipping through the gap between top and curtains.

Then my brother came home for summer vacation.

Then, parked in the driveway, was a Corvette. Dad's new Corvette.

Red, really *red* red, with white inserts and panels, white top, and red interior. Four headlights. Streaks and spears of chrome plating.

This was 1959, when there was nothing excessive about excess, you could say, so the fact that dad's 'Vette was awfully big for two people, and was bright enough to make you blink, was part of the times.

Equally, the 1959 was not on technology's cutting edge. Dad's new car had drum brakes, live rear axle, and springs and shock absorbers chosen to prove the wisdom of Maurice Olley, the man who invented GM's independent front suspension, and the man who said: "Any suspension will work . . . if you don't let it."

None of this mattered. Soon as I saw the car I asked dad "Stick or automatic?" and he gave me the look such a question deserved.

"Stick. That's the whole point."

And I guess it was. Dad never raced or rallied, and I'd bet never actually wound the engine into the sports zone but that, too, wasn't the point. They were having fun. The noise and rough ride were part of the fun, and the 283 V-8 was (in secret) a sedan engine, as reliable and as good a consumer product as was ever offered by the free market.

Then I went off to school, the mileage on dad's 'Vette got into six figures, and I suppose he could have had an attack of late maturity, cause he sold the Corvette to my younger brother and got . . . a Mercedes-Benz coupe.

It wasn't the same.

Two New Generations

Fast forward to 1963. Chevrolet has become serious about the Corvette. Zora Arkus-Duntov, who needs no introduction here, has been hired, and the engineers have provided disc brakes and independent rear suspension, while Bill Mitchell and his stylists have done a classic shape and the perfect name, Sting Ray.

There's racing stuff and, well, street racing stuff and options for engine and transmission and bodies, coupe or convertible. The coupe has a trademark, the divided rear window, and if it's a clear victory of form over fashion, it's also a feature the public will notice and still remark forty years later.

This is a better Corvette, as well as being a smaller and more agile Corvette, and there are those who still see the Sting Ray as the peak of the marque.

Meanwhile, yrs truly has had a maturity attack of his own, becoming a husband and father while still in school, keeping the MG-TC and acquiring a disabled old Lotus to be reworked and raced.

My help in this (ultimately doomed) venture was a neighbor, a physician just beginning his residency at a nearby hospital. He had a second bay in the garage behind his condo, and he let me park the Lotus parts there.

Also, he had a Sting Ray, a white coupe.

My second son was barely walking about this time, but he was old enough that, when we'd have an errand, he could clamber into the Corvette, along with his sister and big brother.

Dr. Sam and I would be in the seats, of course, while the little kids would perch on the leading edge of the parcel shelf behind the seats, and no, there were no kiddie seats or seatbelts back there—what can I say, who knew?

Anyway, it would have spoiled the fun. We'd come to an open stretch, Dr. Sam would punch it, and the fuel-injection moaned as the coupe leapt forward and the kids rolled into the back of the cabin, giggling like the little fiends they were.

We did this every chance we got, and like so many childish games, it never got old.

There was another feature to the Sting Ray.

For ostensible aerodynamic purposes, the headlights were concealed. During daylight their assemblies rotated, so the lights were inside, and the front was a wind-splitting peak. Hit the switch and they rolled out.

Son John was literally fascinated. Every chance he got, he gestured to the patient doctor and the lights went in . . . out . . . in . . . out.

"Sting Ray," John said every time, "Sting Ray."

His mom doesn't agree, but my version of history says his first words were . . . "Sting Ray."

Big Brother, Big Block

My older brother, meanwhile, developed a case of early maturity. He finished college and went off to seek his fortune in the west. OK it was Ohio, which is west only to New Englanders. But he sold the Healey and drove dumb sedans on business.

He was promoted to the head office, in Manhattan, and moved back into his childhood home when mom and dad built their retirement cottage.

And he got his own Corvette.

This was 1975, and there had been lots of progress.

The big block had arrived, along with independent suspension front and rear, and by that time, the looks had gone from garish to confrontational.

The 1975 Corvette was as in-your-face as any two-seat ever has been. It was big, make that bulky, with an aggressive front, and it came as a coupe or a convertible, both aerodynamic.

Impressive.

Fashions, almost by definition, are in a state of constant change, and in 1975, the convertible, in general, had gone from every man's dream to a waste of air conditioning. The market had stopped dead, and there was

talk of government action on the grounds of safety.

Model Year 1975 was the last for convertibles, General Motors said, so that's what my older brother bought.

Orange. Hang on, that's not enough emphasis, it was ORANGE, a deep rich shade, and as soon as one's eyes had processed that, there were the sidepipes, the exhaust outlets dumping fumes (presumably) and sound (undeniably) for all the world to know about.

The convertible could be bought with a removable hardtop, which one slung from the rafters when not on the car, then lowered into place. It wasn't, or so my dad and brother told me, as much bother as it looked.

Not that my brother would have cared. He's not a competition type; he went to driver's school and decided he'd rather be a fan.

But the Corvette was his delight, and he never minded taking every step in the maintenance manual, or covering the car when it was in the garage, or ritually swapping tops spring and fall.

Then, trouble. A mysterious ache turned out to be cancer, and it cost him a leg.

"Oh, no," I said, thinking seriously of all the problems.

"It's not that bad," he said, "I found a guy who can swap the four-speed for an automatic."

Which is what they did, and my brother drove the car for fifteen more years.

When we'd go someplace and he pulled into the handicap spot, I used to say "Oh, geez, get outta here, you'll get a ticket."

He'd whack his artificial leg with his cane, reminding me of what I'd forgotten, but the truth is, guys like my brother may be slowed down, but they aren't handicapped.

Dawn of the Corvette

A 1954 Corvette glows at dawn's first light. The Blue Flame Six engine fathered just 150 hp, although power was increased to 155 hp partway through the 1954 production run due to a camshaft redesign. It wasn't much, but the Corvette had more style than any other American car on the road in its day. (Photograph © Jerry Heasley)

Overleaf:
Star-Spangled Sports Car

A 1967 Corvette convertible poses in front of an American flag. (Photograph © Lucinda Lewis/All Rights Reserved)

Adventures in Flint

By Mike Antonick

After graduating from General Motors Institute in 1970, Mike Antonick worked for GM, then Booz-Allen & Hamilton management consultants, then General Electric. It was while at GE that Mike decided to take a break from the engineering grind and publish some Corvette books. He came up with a hardbound subscription series called *Corvette! The Sensuous American.* His intent was to do three books per year for three years, period. But one thing led to another, and all these years and nearly a million books later, he's still at it.

Mike is best known for his *Corvette Black Book,* a 160-page, pocket-sized bible of Corvette facts that is updated annually. When the Corvette hit its fiftieth birthday in 2003, Mike's *Corvette Black Book* reached its twenty-fifth.

Despite owning and driving countless Corvettes over the years, nothing can ever match the memories of that first one. In *Adventures in Flint,* Mike recalls a series of events—all true, he swears—surrounding his first Corvette.

Facing page:
Hot Rodders
Two hot rodders share tuning notes in this vintage image with a 1965 Corvette convertible alongside Junior's miniature rod. (Photograph © Jerry Irwin)

Inset:
1963 Corvette Brochure

In his book, *Chrysler: The Life and Times of an Automotive Genius*, Vincent Curcio writes that Walter Chrysler's first foray into the automotive world came as works manager of the Buick factory in Flint, Michigan. It seems unusual that a job of such magnitude and responsibility would drop into Walter Chrysler's novice lap, but he'd already established himself as one of the nation's great railroad men. His $6,000 annual starting salary at Buick—not bad in 1912—was a 50 percent cut from what he left behind at American Locomotive Company. Chrysler gambled on the automobile's future and figured the money would come in time.

By 1916, Chrysler was Buick's president, earning $500,000 a year plus lucrative stock options. After he resigned in 1919, William Durant bought Chrysler's GM stock for a cool $10 million.

It appears Chrysler was worth it. Buick's 1911 production was 13,389. It hit 124,834 in 1916 before World War I intervened. Buick earned $46 million in 1916, fully half of GM's total profit. Plus, Walter Chrysler was a tireless civic leader in Flint, leading a drive for big, high-quality projects to provide housing for Flint's exploding work force. Odd, isn't it, that someone named Chrysler played so key a role in Flint's emergence as one of the most significant cities in GM's early history?

Flint is also important for another reason. It's where I bought my first Corvette.

The purchase itself wasn't memorable. The year was 1966 and the car was a Daytona Blue, 1963 convertible. The owner parked it in his front yard with a For Sale sign taped to the windshield. I looked it over, took it for a spin, and agreed to the $1,650 asking price. No problem, no drama. That came a few weeks later.

Like most red-blooded American males, a Corvette was always on my wish list, but not necessarily at the top. My car-loving friends and I divided into different camps as we grew up, arguing the pros and cons of cars we were years away from owning or driving. I tilted toward the snooty, *Road & Track*, foreign-is-better side of the equation. My first sports car was a 1963 MG-B.

Purchase of Corvette *numero uno* happened while I was enrolled at General Motors Institute (GMI) in Flint. At the time, GMI was a five-year, cooperative engineering college. The "cooperative" part meant students rotated six weeks of school with six weeks of work at a GM facility.

"Marty's Diner"
The 1950s never looked so good as in artist Kent Bash's image of a classic diner and classic cars. (Artwork © Kent Bash)

This was a terrific, inexpensive route to a degree. During the work sessions—usually in different departments each rotation—students were hourly rate employees and well paid. With a little overtime, enough could be earned for tuition, room and board, and other school expenses. I'd worked a few years after high school, diligently putting money aside for college. Finagling my way into GMI let me divert some of my stash to cars, including the MG.

The little British car didn't set well with my Fisher Body sponsor, however. Nothing mattered at the school: beards, casual dress, and any sort of wheels were tolerated. But during work sessions, it was clean shave, white shirt and tie, and a proper car since students parked in the salaried lot. It was made clear to me that non-GM wouldn't cut it, and I saw their point. Besides, Corvette moved into first place on my wish list with the debut of the 1963 Sting Ray. It just hadn't been affordable. With four years of depreciation, the time was right.

GMI still exists, except now it's called Kettering Institute, and GM is but one of many firms sponsoring students. The curriculum—industrial, electrical, or mechanical engineering—was difficult, and the school wasn't coed when I enrolled. A great party school? Not even close.

Trying to help, GMI would occasionally stage a dance at its gym, sending invitations to Flint's Hurley School of Nursing. One blustery Friday evening in December, less than a month after acquiring my pride-and-joy first Corvette, Tim Harrington—my best fraternity friend—and I decided to check out one of these gym dances. Our fraternity house was in a neighborhood three miles from campus that had once been grand but was now down on its luck. As we neared the school on a narrow, one-way residential street, a huge Buick (Flint still has loads of 'em) backed out of a private driveway right into my path. I swerved left, but caught the Buick's left rear with my Corvette's right front. It was a glancing blow, but enough to bend my bumper, aim my headlight pod at the stars, and bust my fender. While the Buick driver—a municipal court judge, of all the luck—called the police from his house, Tim and I gathered up fender debris. In my naïveté, I thought I could jigsaw-puzzle it back together. Heck, the pieces were all there. The judge returned and announced that since both cars could be driven and nobody was injured, the police wouldn't come. We should exchange information and let our insurance companies sort it out.

Tim—the eternal optimist—thought things could only improve after this and suggested we mosey on to the dance. He had a feeling.

We entered to the usual grim scene—GMI guys standing around, trying to act oblivious of the lucky few who'd managed to glom onto a girl. It looked hopeless, but Tim's antenna acquired a signal.

"Hold on. Our dates for the evening have just arrived," he assured me.

As best friends, Tim and I had long since worked out a system to avoid arguments about who attempted to get which girl. I disliked smoking intensely. Tim didn't smoke, but wasn't bothered by it. Tim wasn't bothered by much of anything. Except gum. Gum chewing, especially gum-chewing, laughing, talking, giggling . . . well, something in the synergy of all that jaw action drove him bonkers. I didn't care. So we'd observe candidates until one of these traits manifested itself.

The girls who'd set off Tim's radar had just entered. The blonde was lighting up and the brunette was blowing gum bubbles. Tim made a beeline for the smoke, and before other GMI-ers can react, he's helping with her coat.

"Jeeze, it's about time you two got here. We almost left. What's your name again?"

"I'm Diane. Who are you?"

"I'm Tim, and this is Mike. But look, if your friend there has any designs on him, tell her to forget it. A judge just bashed into his Corvette and he's not in the mood."

To this point, the brunette, Rita, hadn't made eye contact with me or any of the other cretins in the gym. She had an indifferent, don't-waste-your-time-with-me aura, but the word "Corvette" sliced right into her cerebellum, activating circuits. She ceased chewing and spoke softly.

"I'm so sorry to hear about your accident. You poor thing. Are you okay? Is your car okay?

"Thank you. Yes. Yes, well, it's mangled a little."

"Is it really a Corvette?

In a sea of dweebs, the Corvette dweeb gets the girl.

She wanted to see the Corvette, so outside we go. Even crunched, the Corvette was the best-looking car in the lot. Before long, Tim, Diane, and Rita agree I'd feel better with some food, so we cram into the Corvette and head off to a local Italian restaurant-pizza-sub joint.

You haven't lived until you've doubled in a Corvette. The driver's date straddles the console. It helps if she can shift. The passenger's date sits on his lap. This is a good ice breaker.

The restaurant was one of our regular hangouts. Gourmet it wasn't, but portions were generous, which counted for a lot. We settled into a booth amid approving glances, thumbs up, and assorted gestures from dateless GMI-ers at the bar. It could have been a *Gunsmoke* scene at Miss Kitty's Longbranch Saloon, except these gunslingers had slide rules in their holsters.

Rita surveys the menu and announces she'll have the spaghetti platter. Tim and I chuckle and explain that the spaghetti platter is huge! Maybe the petite portion?

Rita rolls her eyes. "Oh, great. Mister big-shot Corvette man can't afford a bowl of pasta. This is looking like a major mistake. Maybe one of you guys at the bar knows how to treat a lady?"

The waiter took this in, and when Rita asked his opinion, he replied in his best Italian-French-Flint accent, "I believe madam deserves *vatever* she desires."

Fine.

The rest of us decided to share a pizza. Tim and Diane got along splendidly. Rita and I mostly listened to them. As Tim described *his* car, an ex–Delaware State Police Ford repainted camouflage olive drab, the food arrived.

The waiter strained under the weight of a spaghetti platter twice its normal heft, a foot-high Vesuvius topped by a grapefruit-sized meatball. The waiter deposited this load on our table, then doubled over in laughter as the whole restaurant cracked up.

I thought she'd storm out, but Rita took a different tact. Pretending it was exactly what she expected, she fanned a little spaghetti steam toward her face and purred, "Smells wonderful. Let's eat." She made a valiant effort, chipping the meatball in half and carving a noticeable wedge in the pasta. It took the restaurant's biggest take-home box to hold the remains.

Corvettes lost their external trunk lids in 1963. The luggage compartment was an open bay behind the seats, accessed from inside. There's a depressed area right

behind the seats which would have been the perfect spot to stow the spaghetti, but I shoved it all the way to the rear thinking it stayed like a refrigerator back there. This explains why, when I had to slam the brakes to avoid a pussycat tiptoeing across Dort Highway, the spaghetti got good launch velocity before detonating into a seatback.

Saturday dawned brisk and bright, and I resolved it would be a better day. Our fraternity president, a wise old senior, owned a solid-axle Corvette and gave me directions to a local body shop steeped in the mysteries of fiberglass. I phoned my insurance agent, explained it wasn't my fault, but that the police refused to investigate. He said I should have gotten an investigation somehow but, given the situation, my insurance would pay to fix the Corvette. The judge was on his own.

As someone who attempts to maintain a glass-half-full attitude, my noggin started formulating a plan to turn this lousy chain of events into something positive.

Remember, all this happened late in 1966. My 1963 Corvette was the first of the Sting Ray mid-year models; the 1967 just released a few months earlier was the last. Chevy brought the big-block engine option to Corvettes in 1965. Big-block Corvettes had different hoods than small-block models, and 1967's was unique to it. I loved that hood and I wanted one on my '63. My hood wasn't damaged by the accident and was fine except for a little paint lifting around the fake louver depressions, a common problem. I figured my insurance company could pay the body shop a fair price for repairing and refinishing the collision damage, but I'd work a side deal for leaving the repairs in primer to offset switching hoods. Then I'd repaint the whole car myself. I had repainted my first car, a stylish 1954 Studebaker coupe, with a Sears compressor and Binks gun right on my mom's gravel driveway. That was three years earlier, and I'd chosen—you guessed it—1963 Corvette Daytona Blue paint. For as long as the Bondo held, it looked magnificent.

With the quality of Corvettes today, and the gorgeous restorations of older models we see at shows, it is easy to forget the paint from the factory in the "old days" wasn't so hot. The St. Louis Corvette assembly plant always struggled with those darn bonding seams between exterior body panels, a curse finally banished

"Granny Grabbingears"
Vince Crain was inspired by the 1960's Rat Fink artwork of Ed "Big Daddy" Roth, Dave Deal, and CARtoons magazines in creating his modern-day images of outrageous hot-rodded cars. This 1964 Candy Apple Red 'Vette is driven by Granny only to church on Sundays—via a special shortcut down the neighborhood dragstrip. (Artwork © Vince Crain)

starting with 1984 models by just designing them out. Considering it was in its fifth Michigan winter, my Corvette's exterior was pretty decent. Still, it was beginning to show stress cracks and chips. The interior was A-1. So with a repaint and a '67 big-block hood, it would take a pro to know my Corvette wasn't brand new.

The body shop manager was a good guy and willing to go along with my plan but, alas, leaving the repaired area in primer didn't save enough to offset the cost of the new hood, even allowing for my old one in trade. I'd have to pony up additional funds. I said I'd think about it.

My mind was working the problem as I drove back to the fraternity. Within two blocks of the house, my peripheral vision detected an old Buick (what else?) lumbering in from the left, with a two-headed driver. Surely he's going to stop . . .

I stabbed the brakes and almost missed him, but an instant later he glanced off my left front. Now the Corvette's right side damage from the previous evening was almost perfectly matched by new damage to the left.

The two-headed driver turned out to be a middle-aged guy with a very underage girlfriend on his lap, blocking his sight line to the stop sign he'd just driven through. Some fraternity brothers heard the crash and trotted over. I told them to make sure the cars stayed put. I headed back to the house to call this in myself.

"Flint Police Department."

"I'd like to report an accident. My car is disabled and my leg's probably broken."

The medics weren't happy with my speedy recovery, but the policeman was on my side. With the Buick driver blaming the whole thing on his way-too-young companion, I could read the anger in the policeman's eyes. He wrote a report and cited Mr. Buick.

The body shop manager was outside writing another estimate when I pulled back in just before noon that same morning. I remember the look on his face, but words fail me.

The Corvette got the big-block hood and was left in primer from the firewall forward. When the weather warmed several months later, I sanded the rest of the body and laid down a splendid nitrocellulose lacquer paint job.

I was by then thoroughly bitten by the Corvette bug. This car set off a love affair with Corvettes I still enjoy today. Since it looked so good, I decided to sell the 1963 and parlay a small profit into a newer model. That would be a 1964 convertible, black, with black and white interior. Then a 1965 coupe, a 1966 convertible, a 1967 coupe . . . and on and on.

A gent in my hometown, Mike Compton, bought the 1963 and never sold it. He enjoyed the car for years, eventually painting it gold, adding fender flares and big tires, and doing a little amateur racing. His son Todd, a toddler when the Corvette arrived, grew up with the car. A few years ago, Mike gave him the Corvette. Todd is a custom home builder, with a reputation such that whenever one of his houses is later on the market, ads always mention who built it. He turned the same quality instincts to the Corvette, doing a body-off restoration and taking the car back to factory-new condition. So the hood I went to so much trouble getting is now on some 1967 where it belongs. To equalize his garage, Todd bought a 1963 split-window coupe—Daytona Blue, of course—built within days of the convertible, and restored it to the same level.

Chip Miller, the cofounder and co-owner of Carlisle Productions, the company behind those great car shows in Pennsylvania each year, likes to say the Corvette hobby isn't about the cars, but about the people the cars bring together. He's absolutely right, but I'd add to the mix the stories and memories that swirl around the people and their Corvettes.

Be careful in Flint, though.

Destination

Route 66 ends at Santa Monica Pier, jutting out into the Pacific Ocean along the California coast. A 1966 Corvette convertible finishes its journey west as a 1966 Shelby Mustang GT350 sets out for the eastern horizon. (Photograph © Lucinda Lewis/All Rights Reserved)

Hymns to the Corvette

Rock'n'roll and Corvettes were made for each other. From both the dawn of rock and the debut of the Corvette, it was only a matter of time before someone united the two in song.

California surf music and the numerous hot-rod anthems of groups like The Beach Boys and Jan and Dean sang tributes to Corvettes in their supercharged car songs. Yet it was Prince in 1983 with his rock'n'roll love song "Little Red Corvette" that made the rocking 'Vette the most famous on radios around the world.

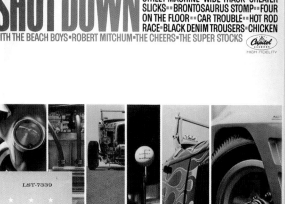

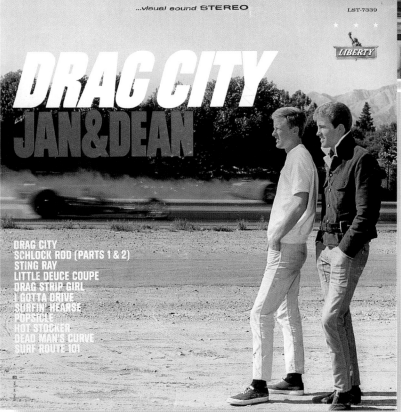

"Shut Down"

Hot-rodded 1960s rock'n'roll collections like "Shut Down" were chockfull of hymns to Corvettes and other muscle cars. Actor Robert Mitchum's "The Ballad of Thunder Road" was a perennial fave, as were the numerous car tunes by The Beach Boys.

Jan & Dean

Jan Berry and Dean Torrence were surf music and hot-rod anthem hotshots in the 1960s. Their Drag City LP was packed with Corvette tunes, from "Drag Strip Girl" to "Sting Ray," but it was their gas-fueled melodrama "Dead Man's Curve," featuring a drag-racing 'Vette, that streaked to number eight on the U.S. pop music charts in 1964.

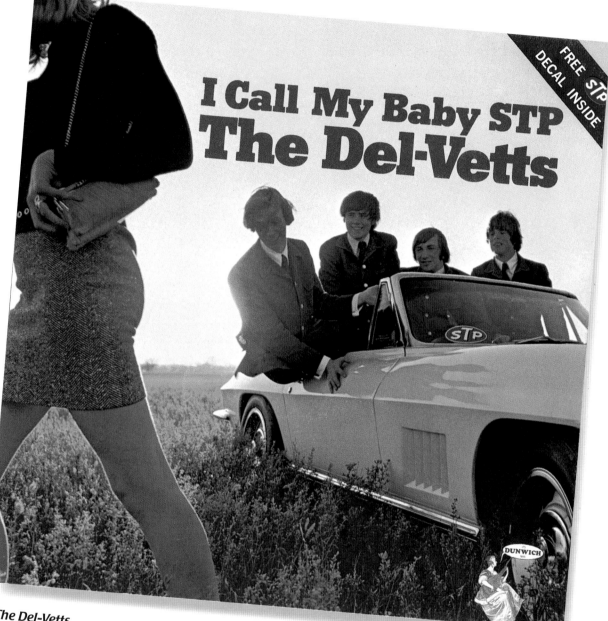

The Del-Vetts

The Del-Vetts formed in 1964 playing Chuck Berry covers for rich white kids in Chicago. Their 45-rpm single "I Call My Baby STP" became a cult hot-rod anthem, although it seemed an odd thing to call your baby. This single came complete with your very own STP sticker—perhaps to slap across your baby's forehead.

★ ★ ★

Getting Your Kicks
on Route 66

By Martin Milner

Many people remember the 1960–1964 television show *Route 66* for the starring role played by a Chevrolet Corvette. But the man at the wheel of that Corvette was actor Martin Milner as the character Tod Stiles.

Martin also starred in the long-running TV series *Adam-12* as well as a list of movies as long as your arm, from 1957's *Gunfight at the O.K. Corral* to 1967's *Valley of the Dolls*, as well as the Mamie Van Doren classic *Sex Kittens Go to College.*

But it was for his role in *Route 66* that Martin is best remembered by Corvette fans. Here, in this vintage interview, he recalls getting his kicks on Route 66.

Facing page:
Route 66 Glory Days
George Maharis as Buz Murdock, left, and Martin Milner as Tod Stiles rest on their trusty Corvette that carried them the length and breadth of Route 66 in search of adventure on the classic television series. The show was a modern-day western with the do-good heroes accompanied by their trusty steed, in the time-honored vein of Roy Rogers and Trigger or Gene Autry and Champion.

Inset:
1959 Corvette Brochure

I was born in Michigan, but I was raised out West. I've lived in Seattle, San Francisco, Los Angeles, and San Diego, so I'm actually a westerner at heart. I think that came across in the television show I starred in called *Route 66*, which aired from 1960 until 1964, and, I suppose, will always be playing on some channels. My character in *Route 66* was named Tod Stiles. George Maharis played a fellow named Buz Murdock. Later, Glenn Corbett took over the other role for a while when Maharis dropped out because of a bout with hepatitis.

The program was created by Sterling Silliphant and Herbert Leonard, who had cast Maharis in an episode of their hit show *Naked City*. From what I know, Silliphant said, "Why don't we put together a show about two guys riding around the country in a car?" The idea was for everybody to rediscover the United States through our characters' eyes.

Route 66 was very symbolic. It represented the spirit of movement and adventure in the country. It was a natural. From the very beginning the show had a great following and became very popular.

I tried to talk them out of using a Corvette in the show. I did my best to convince them to use something really exotic. I said, "Let's get a Ferrari. A Corvette is too ordinary." Remember, I'm a Californian and I was used to seeing 'Vettes. To me a Ferrari was really something special. But we went with Chevrolet and used Corvettes. It was the perfect vehicle.

The car we used on the show changed every year. Chevrolet was always very anxious to show their new products. The first year of the show came to an end and we were getting set for the second year, and they didn't want us to use the same '59 Corvette. They really wanted us to have a new 1960 model. So Sterling wrote a show where we crashed the car, saving some rich man's life, and the man turned around and replaced our Corvette with a new model, and everybody was happy. Every year after that, we got a brand new model for the show but there were no more crashes in the scripts. We just changed cars each season and that was it. Nothing was ever said.

Of the two characters, the one I played, Tod Stiles, was the more intellectual. He came from a well-to-do family and was college educated, optimistic, and a liberal who always believed in doing things the right way. Beneath everything, Tod felt that people could be trusted, and that everything was going to be just fine.

He had a great deal of compassion and integrity. Stiles was more carefree. He had inherited some money from his father in order to buy that first Corvette.

Now Buz, on the other hand, was a real street kid. He was a bad boy from the ghetto—from Hell's Kitchen—and had been involved in crime. His adopted father had died in his arms from an overdose, and Buz had truly seen the worst part of life. He was suspicious and didn't trust anyone. The characters were very different and that made for a great show. There was balance. Also, there was some awfully good writing. The top-notch writing, direction, and the casting were very critical in that show's success.

The funny thing is we hardly did any real location

Power in Style

Just sixteen 1967 L71 Corvettes were fitted with the optional L89 aluminum-alloy cylinder heads, aiding the 427-ci (6,994-cc) V-8 to produce its 435 hp in style. The L89 option cost just $368.65 in 1967, but is worth thousands today due to its incredible rarity. (Photograph © Jerry Heasley)

work out on Route 66. The show was named after the highway, but we did most of the filming elsewhere. It was nothing against the highway, but we just wanted to keep it neat and clean and convenient, so when the weather was good, we'd be near the East Coast and when the weather was lousy we'd be in Florida or Texas or Arizona. We did some work up in the Pacific Northwest and we filmed around Chicago and Pittsburgh,

too. We cruised the highway in our shiny Corvette and came into everybody's living room every Friday night. Along the way we met Robert Redford, Alan Alda, Robert Duvall, Rod Steiger, Gene Hackman, Lee Marvin, Cloris Leachman, Jean Stapleton, and a lot of other talented folks.

For a hundred and sixteen episodes Tod and Buz tooled along *Route 66*. It was great adventure.

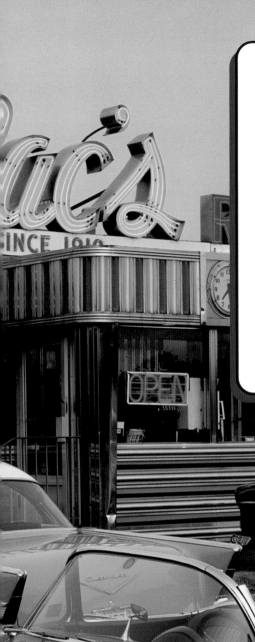

CHAPTER 3

Corvette Fever

Al Mac's Diner
The parking lot is often full at Al Mac's Diner in Fall River, Massachusetts, including a 1958 Corvette convertible. Built by the DeRaffle Manufacturing Company of New Rochelle, New York, Al Mac's is crowned by a tiara of magnificent neon. (Photograph © Lucinda Lewis/All Rights Reserved)

Own America's Number One Fun Car
RIGHT NOW!

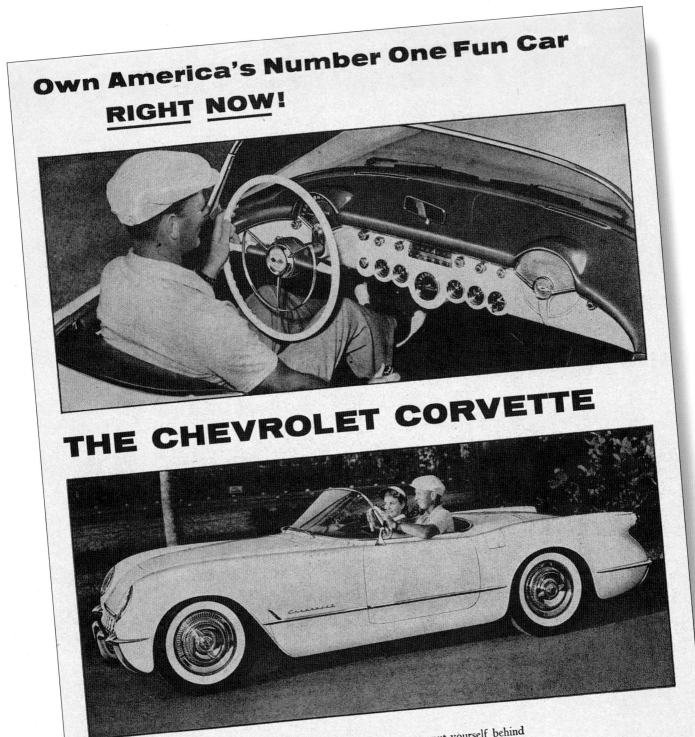

THE CHEVROLET CORVETTE

Simply see your Chevrolet dealer and place your order. It's that easy to put yourself behind the wheel of a Corvette. And what a thrill is waiting for you in the performance of the Corvette's special 150-horsepower "Blue-Flame" engine... in its luxurious, low-lined beauty (33-inch height at door top)... in its compact maneuverability (102-inch wheel base)... and in the sports car roadability of its outrigger type rear springs and wide 57-inch front tread. A Corvette can be yours as soon as you wish, and can be serviced wherever you go. See your Chevrolet dealer. . . . Chevrolet Division of General Motors, Detroit 2, Michigan.

First of the dream cars to come true

The Good Old Days: My Corvette Story

By Noland Adams

Noland Adams needs little introduction to serious Corvette fans. He is the author of the Corvette restorer's bible, *The Complete Corvette Restoration & Technical Guide–Vol. 1: 1953 Through 1962*, and its sequel, *The Complete Corvette Restoration & Technical Guide–Vol. 2: 1963 Through 1967*.

In addition, Noland has penned several hundred magazine articles and five books on Corvette history covering the years 1953 to 1960. He has also hosted a videotape series and has given presentations on Corvette restoration all over the United States as well as in Canada, Sweden, and England.

Noland lives with his second wife, Mary, who supported him during the writing of the 1963–1967 guide. They live in the Sierra foothills east of Sacramento.

In this essay, Nolan reminisces about his introduction to the Corvette world and the inspiration for writing his first book.

Facing page:
The Good Old Days
"Own America's Number One Fun Car—Right Now!" shouted this October 1954 advertisement for the Corvette that appeared in automobile and other magazines across the United States.

Inset:
1962 Corvette Brochure

I was born on January 18, 1933, in Central California. In school I was socially backwards and achieved next to nothing. I was trying to make a go of it in junior college when I was drafted on January 30, 1953. The Korean War ended while I was in basic training, so I was shipped to Europe where I spent one and a half years as a Jeep and truck driver.

I always liked cars. Just before I was drafted I had a 1932 Ford three-window coupe that had an extreme chopped top and a suicide front end. The engine, as with all hot rods of the time, was a flathead V-8 Ford. The engine had been stroked, ported, and relieved, fitted with finned aluminum heads, and mounted with three Stromberg two-barrel 97 carburetors. In 1951 and 1952, it was a state-of-the-art engine.

So I carried my love for cars to France. One of my friend's parents was thoughtful, sending me copies of all the current car magazines. I recall *Motor Life* especially. I read about the new cars and the dream cars, and passed the magazines around to others to enjoy.

My two years were up in January 1955, and I happily returned to civilian life. My parents rewarded me with the gift of a 1950 Chevrolet two-door sedan. Since I had no other wheels, I was glad to get it. However, it was bright blue outside and bright red inside; I decided to grin and bear the color combination. The roads were just being upgraded to freeways, and the speed limit was still 55. However, this Chevy had the typical closed driveline with a problem. At 50 mph it demonstrated an imbalance that doubled with every mile-per-hour over 50. The local auto parts store had a sleeve that was inserted in the rear of the transmission to settle down the driveline vibration. It helped a little, but I was destined to drive the rest of my days under 50 mph!

Then I got a job at Standard Stations cleaning windows and pumping gas. One day in April 1955, I was on the afternoon shift, and my kid brother Lane and I were out looking at cars in Modesto. We wandered into Elmo's Used Cars and started looking around. The owner came out and casually mentioned that he had a Corvette out back that was for sale. There it was, a 1954 Corvette in perfect condition and less than a year old. The price? Only $2,250. Well, I was working and living at home, which meant no rent to pay. The blue-and-red Chevy was only five years old, and it would be the down payment.

Only an hour before, I had read about the Corvette and the other dream cars. But I had never been

close enough to a Corvette to touch one, and tomorrow I would own one. The next morning I was at the dealer's bright and early. Not only did I get rid of that vibrating old Chevy, but also in addition I had a like-new Chevrolet Corvette!

Up to this point I was pretty much ignored by the local girls. But with a Chevrolet Corvette, it was different. No one said just "Corvette" in those days; you always used the full title, "Chevrolet Corvette." For some reason, girls liked to be seen in the Chevrolet Corvette, and suddenly I had a few to pick from. Now, those were the good old days.

The new Chevrolet V-8 was all the talk around.

Bulging Hood

The L78 option package provided a 396-ci (6,486-cc) V-8 stuffed between that special bulging hood and 425 hp on tap. The big-block arrived in mid March 1965 and was fitted to just 2,157 Corvettes that year, including this 396 convertible. (Photograph © Jerry Heasley)

I decided I wanted to learn about the V-8 version of the Chevrolet Corvette. So in June I went back to Modesto, this time to Helm Chevrolet. Although this was a fairly large dealer, they had no information on the 1955 V-8 Corvette at all. They called the zone office, and I learned that the body style was unchanged, and exterior colors were available. It seemed the dealer was satisfied selling conservative six-cylinder sedans.

A two-seat, plastic-bodied sports car was beyond their understanding.

The Chevrolet Corvette was always the talk of the true car guys, however. One who stopped by was named Brad and he lived in Stockton. He went home and told his parents that he wanted a new Corvette. His folks replied that they didn't want him in any of those little foreign cars. He informed them that the Corvette was built by Chevrolet right in the good old USA. The next day his father walked into Chase Chevrolet in Stockton and ordered a new V-8 Corvette. I saw it later—it was white with a Powerglide transmission—but soon after that Brad and his 1955 Corvette moved on.

Near the end of summer I had a steady girlfriend. As I took her home in the country, I drove a newly completed road. Suddenly, we slid on gravel, drifted off the road and right into a telephone pole. The Corvette was a total loss. The steering wheel hit my right femur with so much force that it broke the bone. The girl with me suffered the most because she had a compound fracture of the left ankle. That was the worst part of the accident. The date was October 30, 1955.

I got a pin in my leg and was able to walk on crutches. I was getting around pretty good by the end of November. Since I had worked in the family business for years, my father agreed to replace the Corvette. We looked around and found a used '54 in the San Francisco *Chronicle* for $1,950. We drove to San Francisco to look at it, my father bought it for me, and I drove it home. As I looked closer at the car, the doors, hood, trunk, and fold top lid cover didn't fit quite as well. And it just didn't run as strong as my old Corvette. Still, I was quite satisfied. Finally the pink slip ownership document came in the mail, and it was time to register the car. This was a bit confusing, because it was registered as a 1954 using the engine number—instead of the serial number—as the identification number.

I thought I had purchased a 1954 Corvette, but it was determined that the Corvette was a late-1953 model, serial number E53F001284, sold in 1954. It was now April 1955, and I didn't want a *two*-year-old Corvette, so I told most everyone it was a '54, which made it only one year old. I simply did not want an *old* Corvette!

In 1956, I loaned the '53 to a friend to take his girlfriend home. He decided to make a quick left turn, but instead he slid off the road into a light pole. The right rear of the body was destroyed. This guy didn't have any money, so I took it home to repair it myself. Some friend! He never came over again, and I never saw him again.

Fiberglass repair was a new experience back then. I got some material at a boat repair shop and started piecing it together. Actually, at the time it looked pretty good. I even painted it black in my backyard. It looked okay, and I even got a photo of it published in the letters column in *Hot Rod* magazine.

Through a friend, I met my first wife, Sharon. We were married on January 18, 1958. I had been working on a deal to buy a wrecked 1957 Corvette that belonged to a used car lot. The deal went through, and I bought the '57 on January 17, 1958, the day before I was married.

That '57 was Arctic Blue with Silver side coves and a red interior. It had a 270-hp engine with a three-speed close-ratio manual transmission, radio, hardtop only, and whitewall tires. The engine was particularly strong, capable of really good acceleration up to fairly high rpm.

I started drag racing the '57, but slicks were only just being developed in 1958, so I ran on street tires. I found the dual-point distributor required new points and special set up on a Sun machine to adjust the points. The dwell time on the points overlapped to get maximum coil saturation time, and it couldn't be done by hand. The flywheel/clutch was a weak spot, and I had seen several clutches blow up at the drags. To avoid such problems, almost every week I pulled the transmission and clutch to examine them and the flywheel for cracks.

The most difficult item to decide was who got to drive which Corvette. We both worked, so we alternated driving the '53 and '57. Now I can look back and see that those were the good old days.

On August 7, 1959, our first child, Kimberly, was born. Ah, such a beautiful child—we were so proud. However, we needed a family car. My 1960 ad to sell or trade the 1953 Corvette was answered by a couple with a young son that had a car to trade. He wanted a sports car, so we traded—I got a 1947 Chevrolet Fleetline two-door sedan in overall good condition. It seemed like a good trade at the time.

The 1957 Corvette became an extra expense, so we traded it at a used car lot—for a 1954 Volkswagen! It seemed like a good trade at the time.

In 1962, we sold the 1947 Chevy and bought a 1957 Chevrolet 210 two-door station wagon with a six-cylinder engine and a three-speed on the column. Our second child, a son, Marty, was born on April 23, 1963. We were equally proud of our new son, as were all the grandparents and other relatives. The four of us cruised around in our '57 station wagon for many years.

In 1969, I saw an ad from a newly formed club, the Vintage Corvette Club of America (VCCA). I called the founder, a turkey farmer named Ed Thiebaud. Our conversation rekindled my interest in Corvettes, and Ed and I became good friends. I decided to try to locate my old Corvette. Although the couple had moved twice, I was able to track them down. Their young son, now a teenager, had taken the Corvette apart to "restore" it.

It hadn't been on the road since 1965, sitting in their backyard full of water, with parts all over the yard and garage. Of prime importance was the fact that the original engine and most of the original parts were there, although all needed repair and restoration. I bought that old Corvette again and the heap of worn-out parts for $700, loaded up the stuff and brought it home. It seemed like a good deal at the time.

I started restoring the Corvette slowly and carefully. I would remove a part or two and begin repair and restoration. But, as long as I had one section out, it was easy to get to the next parts. I reasoned that the parts should be restored together, so I took off more than one sub-assembly at a time. By now I had several devices removed from the car. Then I realized I had lost track of the pieces—now, did that screw fit in this bracket, or did it retain that cover? So I did the only reasonable thing: I put them all in a big box. After all, it would be easy to reinstall them in their proper and original location, I told myself.

I was learning details about the car from Ed's VCCA. Another club, the Classic Corvette Club 1953–1955 was formed, while Ed closed the VCCA and moved away. In time, the National Corvette Restorers Society (NCRS) was formed, and the CCC 1953–1955 went away.

I joined NCRS as soon as I heard about it, becoming one of its earliest members. I started writing articles for the NCRS publication *The Corvette Restorer* in its second issue. Those were tough days, when information was really hard to locate. I went to all of the NCRS meetings I could and took notes about all of the questions that were asked, and how there were few answers.

In 1975, a Corvette picture book called *The Real Corvette: An Illustrated History of Chevrolet's Sports Car* was published. The photos in the book showed improperly restored old Corvettes. Other NCRS members and I made up a list of errors and sent them to the author. He didn't bother to answer, so we began notifying the vendors selling the book that it was full of errors.

Then I got a call from L. Scott Bailey, the publisher of *Automobile Quarterly*. He had seen my notices that the book *The Real Corvette* was full of errors. He was looking for someone to write a book on Corvettes for *AQ* and wanted to know if I was interested. Up until then I had only written a few articles for NCRS's *The Corvette Restorer*.

After a lot of consideration, I felt that I could write at least part of the Corvette book. I contacted several of the folk in the Corvette hobby that I knew. One must remember that Ed Thiebaud had started the emphasis on the restoration of Corvettes about 1969. Although it was now 1975, the real Corvette restoration movement was just beginning to pick up momentum. We had a lot to learn.

I began with the approach that a book written about Corvettes had to be as complete and accurate as possible. I started within my circle of friends, asking each to write specialized sections on subjects like the engine compartment, transmission, suspension, body repair, body fit, interior, and so on. All readily agreed that they could contribute a certain section of the book. I was pleased: The experts were helping me, and soon I would have the first draft of the manuscript ready for review. While I waited for outlines from the experts, I worked on the overall design of the book. It is well over twenty-five years ago that I asked for outlines and manuscripts for the new Corvette book. The first one has not arrived yet, but I'm still waiting.

In the meantime, I had been attending all the NCRS meets I could. I attended the technical sessions where NCRS members were asking detailed questions. Little was known about such things as factory details, and most questions went unanswered. I took lots of notes, lists of the few known facts, and the questions that were left with no solution. If I could answer all, or even most, of those technical questions, it would be a good book.

I mentioned to L. Scott Bailey that I would be coming to the Chicago area to attend an NCRS function. He replied that he grew up with a friend who was now employed in a management position in General Motors, and if I could get to Detroit, he could get me into the restricted files within Chevrolet. This was an exceptional opportunity, and I made plans to go to Detroit after the NCRS show.

Grand Sport Legacy

To honor the history of the five semi-factory lightweight Grand Sport race cars of 1963–1964, Chevrolet launched the special Grand Sport Package RPO Z16 only on its 1996 Corvette. Power came from the higher-compression LT4 350-ci (5,733-cc) engine with 330 hp under the hood. Just 1,000 Grand Sports were built. (Photograph © Jerry Heasley)

I really didn't know what to expect as I prepared to go to Chevrolet. For one thing, everyone who had attempted to get information from Chevrolet was told that no records were kept. As I reported to the Chevrolet Public Relations area, I was expected and had access to everything. I was shown a four-drawer filing cabinet, the source of information for the entire Public Relations Department. With a flourish, the second drawer was pulled open, and I was told "Enjoy!" It was all Corvette stuff, and a lot of it was information that we had been told over and over no longer existed!

There were a number of 8x10 black-and-white photographs in the file, and I was told I could take any copies in the files, as long as I provided a list of the photos I was taking. That's when I learned about the photograph filing system within GM Photographic, using an "X" followed by a series of numbers. Each "X number" referred to a file stored in GM Photographic's records, each file containing between one and 1,000 negatives.

There were several pages of technical information, and I asked for and got copies of the important stuff. Also in the file cabinet were several 4x5 transparencies in plastic sleeves. Transparencies are positives like a slide, which show the correct colors of the objects. Negatives can be made from transparencies, and prints can be made from the negatives. Among the transparencies were several photographs of old Corvettes that had never been released to the public. This, too, was the good stuff that we had been told again and again didn't exist!

Through my contacts with L. Scott Bailey and *Automobile Quarterly*, I was suddenly considered a member of the press. Now I had to learn and follow the rules of the Public Relations Department. I had been supplied copies of documents and photographs—anything I wanted! But I also wanted copies of the transparencies. There were over a dozen, but I carefully selected eight that were "must have" photos. I was told that they represented a substantial cost to Chevrolet—something like $5 each, and they would see if their budget allowed such an expenditure. I went home with several treasures, with hopes of getting copies of the transparencies.

About three weeks had gone by when a package arrived from Chevrolet Public Relations. I could hardly wait, and to my delight, it contained copies of all eight of the color transparencies. The most important of the

images was taken in Los Angeles on the new Harbor Freeway. A black-and-white version of this photo had been circulated for many years, showing many white 1954 Corvettes and several that appeared to be different colors. But in a b&w photo it was impossible to determine the color of the other Corvettes. Finally this transparency proved the existence of 1954 Corvettes painted black and red by the factory. One of my first calls was to my friend Don Mullenhoff, who owned a black car, just to verify that, for the first time, we had proof that the factory did paint some '54s black and his car was, indeed, original. It doesn't seem like a big deal now, but it sure was then.

Since I was writing a regular column for NCRS's *The Corvette Restorer*, I sent the transparencies to John Amgwert, the editor. Since the publication was quarterly, I supplied never-seen-before color images for the front cover for nearly two years. NCRS was growing and learning, and I added a bit with special covers and articles where I could.

Chevrolet Public Relations had a dilemma, which I learned about by accident. One day when I was in the PR offices the personnel was discussing requests for information about old Corvettes. This was in 1976 or 1977, so an "old" Corvette was probably a '64 or '65 or older. Chevrolet PR was receiving requests for information from Corvette owners, and the folks at Chevy PR had no answers. So I referred them to NCRS, which was only too glad to attempt to answer their questions while recruiting a new member to NCRS. This referral to NCRS worked well for the PR folks for many years.

Through contacts (many started with friends in NCRS), I gained access to numerous "hidden" records within Chevrolet. I found there were two ways to get information: 1) Make a direct request through Chevrolet Public Relations, or 2) go in a side door with a friend. I used both methods. While Chevy PR was helpful, they did not have the personnel to do research for me. I used my side-door approach to locate the files and information I wanted. Once that I knew where it was, I requested copies from Chevrolet PR. This system worked well for both of us: I got what I needed, and they used a minimum of personnel time. I was allowed to take or request copies of almost anything, but I was never permitted to remove originals of anything.

Through a couple of friends I worked miracles through the side door. Both of these side-door men were engineers at Chevrolet. Although both are retired,

I am reluctant to reveal their identities, so I'll just call them "A" and "B." Through their efforts, I was able to learn where the "secret" files were and who to contact to get in these restricted areas. My contact through L. Scott Bailey and *Automobile Quarterly* was important, because I gained access to anything I asked for. Well, there were exceptions—I couldn't get into the design studios to see new Corvette development. But I was interested in the old stuff—1953 to 1967 or 1970, and by now it was 1978.

Among the stuff Mr. A got me into was an area called records retention, which included lots of photographs, sales brochures, and all kinds of technical documents, including the Assembly Instruction Manuals (AIM). The AIM is the exploded views of a specific Corvette model (example: 1962) showing the direction of every bolt and washer, identified by part number. The Corvette assembly plant personnel used the AIM as a guide to assemble Corvettes in a standard and proper manner.

In addition, Mr. B was able to help me locate the area where the blueprints were stored. Well, they weren't blueprints, but copies on an aperture card. The aperture card is about the size of an old 3x9-inch IBM card used in early computers. It contains a section about 2x3 inches that is an image of the original blueprint. When I requested a blueprint, the aperture card was pulled from its file and placed in a reader section of a special printer. The image on the aperture card was transferred to a new copy of the blueprint. This was a convenient method of storing thousands of blueprints without storing them on paper, and still having them available for the engineers.

My plans for the Corvette book were beginning to take shape. L. Scott Bailey began to ask about the book. Is it almost done? Can I see an outline? At the same time, however, I was searching for an organizational outline, the backbone of the book. I finally decided to follow the procedure called the Universal Product Code (UPC) as shown in the AIM. That meant separate sections for body assembly, followed by front suspension, brakes, rear suspension, engine, transmission, electrical, and an options section.

In 1978, we decided that the book would provide information to help the owner with technical details and a guide to the correct parts. One difficult decision was where to break the production years. After looking at all the information I was gathering, I thought a 1953–1962 book was best. However, L. Scott Bailey insisted on a 1953–1978 book. I argued that there were few restoration projects for 1963–1967 Corvettes, and no interest in the newer 1972–1978 models. For one thing, the 1977 and 1978 model was new, and restoration would not be on the owner's minds.

I made up my mind that the book would cover 1953–1962, and I worked on that angle, developing the text. Meanwhile, Scott insisted on a 1953–1979 book as we moved into early 1979. I considered a 1953–1979 book, but that really would be silly.

I still traveled to NCRS meets and took notes and black-and-white photographs wherever I went. It became known that I was working on this phantom Corvette book, which was taking three years—and more. Soon there was a running joke in NCRS circles, as everyone asked the same question: "How's the book coming?" I really got tired of hearing that, but all I could say was that I was making progress.

In late 1979, my wife and I were going in different directions, so we got a divorce. About the same time, I got the manuscripts and the photos and the blueprints together to ship to Scott. There were three separate boxes, each shipped about a month apart. That's really a tough time for a would-be author. Years of lonely work and large expenses are represented by the contents of a rather small box, which you are sending off to a stranger. I felt like I was sending my right arm, and I'm right handed. It was truly difficult to ship that first box. Of course it was insured, but what if it were lost and couldn't be found? The other boxes were a bit easier to send off—but not much.

Of course the material I shipped was for a 1953–1962 book, not the 1953–1979 restoration book that Scott wanted. He grumbled, but had a couple of editors get started on it. About that time the book had a name: *The Complete Corvette Restoration & Technical Guide 1953 Through 1962*. Imagine what a 1953–1979 book would have been?

Back about 1977, I was on the NCRS Board of Directors. While there I made two major proposals: First, the club should be expanded to include 1963–1967 Corvettes. At that point we all owned 1953–1962 Corvettes, and we were just getting comfortable learning about these first years. One argument against expansion was that there were no active 1963–1967 restorations in progress. Not even *one*, as far as we knew, indicating a possible lack of interest. Of course, this was true and perhaps no one cared, but I felt we were too limited by stopping at 1962. There were six of us on the board at the time, and after a vote, we were tied at 3–3. We all discussed the proposed expansion, but we were still tied. Then Sam Folz, who was against expansion, had a fine idea: We would admit 1963–1967 Corvettes on a temporary basis for a year. If there were no serious restoration efforts among the 1963–1967 owners, the expansion would be dropped due to lack of interest. If some 1963–1967s were beginning to be restored, we would automatically expand to 1967. Looking back, it seems silly to question interest in the restoration of 1963–1967 Corvettes. But back in 1977, they were just too new to restore on a large scale.

The second suggestion—in 1978, as I recall—was to allow chapters to form. At the time, the NCRS was new, and the Board of Directors (including me) was cautious. The board had absolute control of everything, and it liked the direction the club was headed. The board was hesitant to share control of the club with anyone, especially a local chapter that might decide to form a chapter with different goals. This time we worked smarter by establishing a set of rules, which allowed for the formation of chapters under strict guidelines. The board was permitting the formation of local chapters without giving away too much authority. Fortunately, the expansion to 1967 Corvettes and the formation of chapters have both been successful.

Now it was early 1980, and the book was going through its final editing. Finally, I would have an answer to "How's the book coming?"

When the book was published, I opted to sell copies myself. I ordered a pallet load, which was delivered to my work. (Yes, all this time I had a job as an industrial instrument technician. I worked on automatic controls for a couple of companies. My Corvette activities were on my own time at my own expense.) A major Corvette show was planned for San Mateo, California, about an hour's drive from my house. As a member of the Northern California Chapter of NCRS, my fellow chapter members and I planned the event. There were a couple of highlights there: One was that I had met Zora Arkus-Duntov, the retired Corvette Chief Engineer who had been responsible for many major developments of the early Corvettes. He and his wife, Elfi, were invited to attend, and to our delight, they did. His presence was greatly appreciated.

Another event that occurred that June that was of greater interest to me than anyone else was the availability of my new book. By then I had a 1972 Chevrolet station wagon, which I loaded with my new books. With the help of several chapter members, we set up a booth to sell my books. And they sold like hotcakes. I was so proud. That's where I first found the ego-satisfying honor of autographing a book that I authored!

Since its first publication in 1980, the book has gone through one update, in 1981. There have been many printings as almost every Corvette restorer uses the book as a standard reference.

My last year on the NCRS Board of Directors was 1980, so I had no part in decision making after that. However, NCRS developed many excellent guidelines for the proper restoration of Corvettes. Part of their information came from my books. The troubling part is that they never asked my permission; they just helped themselves. I have always supported NCRS, and I would have granted them permission to use anything, but it still hurts me that they didn't bother to ask.

Besides having the pleasure of signing books and meeting many Corvette owners, I have been in numerous places where the average Corvette owner cannot go. In one instance, Mr. B took me into a file room to look at a list of production figures in a special binder. As a guest within a Chevrolet facility, I was required to wear a bold "Visitor" badge. As I entered this office area, I felt like a monster from outer space, as everyone stopped and stared. I walked along casually like I belonged there. Later, after we had copied the information, I learned that no outside visitor had ever been allowed in that area before.

I was also allowed in special areas within Chevrolet Engineering, the Design building, truck prototype shop, Corvette prototype shop, the GM Proving Grounds at Milford, Michigan, and many file rooms and photograph storage rooms. In addition, I became friends with Zora and Elfi Arkus-Duntov and visited them in their home several times. Sometimes it seemed like the long lonely hours writing the book were wasted but I made up for them later on.

I took six weeks off and just generally goofed off. I went to the movies and just drove around sightseeing, stuff that I had missed for years. Then I started getting organized for the next book, which would cover 1963–1967 Corvettes. But, that's another story.

Over-Customized Corvettes

There's a fine point at which art no longer imitates life, but where art initiates life, becoming an entirely new entity. These "over-customized" Corvettes are relics—even dinosaurs—from another era.

Right:
Custom Corvette Special!
Styles come and go—sometimes thankfully!

Below:
Bad News
This jacked-up four-wheel-drive Corvette was christened "Bad News." It was certainly a good name. (Photograph © Andrew Morland)

Orange Plus

From the wheelie bars forward, this 1972 Corvette was 1970s style personified. The 543-ci (8,894 cc) V-8 and rear slicks were dragstrip ready, but the rear luggage rack seemed an odd addition. (Photograph © Andrew Morland)

Corvette Summer *Corvette*

They were the 1970s after all, and excess was the name of the game in customizing cars. (Photograph © Jerry Heasley)

* * *

Lifestyle of a Corvette Widower

By Barbara Spear

Barbara Spear is the lifeblood behind the Internet's Yankee Lady Corvette Gazette, a website shrine devoted to all things Corvette. Her own prolific writings on Corvettes run the gamut from fictional short stories to profiles of famous Corvette personalities to personal memoirs, such as this confessional piece.

Facing page:
Admiring Glances
A C3 Corvette parked outside of a Pennsylvania covered bridge draws admiring looks from two Amish people in their horse and buggy. (Photograph © Jerry Irwin)

Inset:
1973 Corvette Brochure

My husband is a Corvette widower. In our family, I'm the 'Vette nut. Now, hubby knew I liked Corvettes when he married me, but the depth of my passion didn't manifest itself until several years into our marriage.

It began on a small scale. Every time we passed a 'Vette on the road, I'd ogle and say something like "Mmm, pretty baby!" Aside from a couple of missed turns, that was nothing for hubby to get concerned over.

Then, I began buying and assembling Corvette models. A harmless pastime that only took a few dollars, the kitchen table, and occasionally stunk up the house with paint or glue fumes. Hubby didn't even complain when I relocated his military history paperbacks to make room for my expanding collection of unopened kits. But one thing leads to another. . . .

One winter, I totaled my Sunbird in the freezing rain. A few days later, hubby came home to find me glowing with self-satisfaction.

"I've found a new car," I announced proudly. Hubby began to look suspicious. "Kenny sold me his 'Vette."

To say that hubby was not pleased would be an understatement. It was February in New England. Though a Corvette makes a nice summer car, this would be my only form of transportation. Also, the 'Vette was a 1973 with high mileage that was bound to have problems.

"Are you out of your mind!?" Hubby yelled.

I dug my heels in and replied, "Probably, but I'm buying it anyway! I might never get another chance to buy a 'Vette and I'm not letting this one go by. You know I've wanted Kenny's 'Vette for years."

Needless to say, the rest of hubby's protests fell on deaf ears. The 'Vette was mine.

Of course, hubby was right. The 'Vette was unreliable from the start. It needed lots of repairs. And it always broke down when we could least afford it. My first year as a 'Vette owner put a real strain on my marriage.

Eventually, I bought a winter car so the 'Vette could stay in the garage during bad weather. Since I bought a new Jeep Cherokee, it seemed only natural that it and the 'Vette got places in our two-car garage. Hubby's truck had to stay outside. Fortunately, this did not become a bone of contention.

One chronic sore point has been who can drive my 'Vette. The first time hubby pulled my '73 into the garage, he almost smacked the nose into the wall. I immediately became a raving maniac. Since that outburst, hubby has flatly refused to drive my 'Vette. He won't even move it if it's blocking his truck in the driveway. Though he usually keeps his feelings to himself, if one of our friends accidentally stumbles onto the subject, hubby quickly snaps "I don't drive *her* 'Vette—ever!"

I think hubby hoped that once I owned a 'Vette my passion would be satisfied. Instead, I became interested in attending 'Vette shows. I wanted to buy an owner's manual and a few reference books. Hubby politely accompanied me to one show. He didn't have a terrible time. He helped me find the books I wanted, pointed out a nice Corvette poster, and actually enjoyed reading the silk-screened T-shirts that were for sale. When we got home, he announced that I could go to future shows alone.

Eventually, my passion did ebb a bit, and for a couple of years, I just enjoyed my 'Vette. Hubby was lulled into a false sense of stability. My mechanic, the instigator, rekindled my passion. In a casual conversation, I fantasized that someday, I'd like to own a whole fleet of 'Vettes. My fleet would include a 1953 (since that was the year I was born), a 1963 split-window coupe, my 1973, and a 1978 and/or 1982.

When he returned from the spring show at Carlisle, my mechanic gleefully announced that he'd found a nice 1963 split-window coupe for me in light blue. It was priced at just over $19,000. Very funny. I reminded my mechanic that my finances wouldn't support such an extravagance, then dismissed the idea. I laughingly mentioned the "find" to hubby who didn't worry. He knew that I couldn't and wouldn't pursue a 'Vette at that price. But one thing leads to another. . . .

A few weeks later, the instigator called again. "I've found a '63 for you," he announced jovially.

Tri-Power
A trio of second-generation Corvette coupes—two split-window 1963s in the front and a 1965 bringing up the rear. The C2 Corvette debuted in 1963 with a new chassis featuring independent rear suspension and a stunning new body, based on Bill Mitchell's Stingray race car. Sales almost instantly doubled over the previous year to 21,513 examples. A legend was born. (Photograph © Jerry Heasley)

"I know," I said, "It's light blue and it's $19,000."

"No," he retorted, "it's black, and it's in your price range."

My mechanic then went on to describe this 'Vette, which had been in a fire. The alarm had shorted, but the firewall held, so only the interior was scorched.

He had my attention. I asked to see the 'Vette. I got a run-around.

A few days later, I saw my mechanic and again asked when I could see the '63.

"I want to see it before I decide," I explained.

"Well," he hesitated, "you can see it when it gets here . . . I bought it."

I was livid. How could he buy a 'Vette for me without letting me inspect it first? To diffuse my redhead temper, my mechanic quickly explained that if I didn't want the 'Vette, he'd simply sell it to someone else. All he was offering me was first refusal. I didn't tell hubby.

I did, however, start casually mentioning how nice '63 'Vettes were and how eventually I'd like to add one to my collection.

The '63 arrived in pieces, first the frame and engine, then the body. I started spending a fair amount of time with my mechanic, watching and photographing the first stages of the restoration. As the work progressed, I knew I had to tell hubby.

I went out and bought some tenderloin steaks, baking potatoes, an apple pie, some of hubby's favorite Vermont cheddar cheese, and some gourmet vanilla ice cream. I chilled a bottle of hubby's favorite wine and put a nice new tablecloth on the dining-room table. I was going to put candles on the table, but decided against it. A candlelight dinner would be a dead giveaway that something was up—and since I wasn't pregnant, and no extra dogs would meet him at the door, hubby would probably guess what I'd done.

Hubby arrived home from work late and was so distracted by business problems that he hardly noticed the special meal. I politely listened to his work woes, waiting for the right moment. After serving the hot apple pie with ice cream and a thick wedge of his favorite cheddar, I broke the news as gently as I could and explained carefully that I hadn't committed to buying the 'Vette.

To my surprise, hubby handled the news very well. He reminded me that he always liked the 1960s 'Vettes best. Then he told me that I was on my own as far as financing the 'Vette.

Fortunately for my cash flow, the restoration took longer than anticipated. In the interim, I turned my passion to new directions, such as writing about Corvettes. Hubby's military history books got relocated again to accommodate the many reference books that accumulated in my 'Vette library.

Eventually, I sold my project '63 to a cousin. Hubby was thrilled, figuring my Corvette passion was finally ebbing.

Nope. My Corvette writing and show attendance eventually led me to open my own swap meet on the Internet and begin publishing an e-zine. My online Corvette activities may keep me closer to home and not strain the budget as much, but hubby still has trouble pulling me away from my 'Vettes.

At this point, I think hubby is resigned to the fact that he is a Corvette widower. When my passion for 'Vettes runs high, he just shakes his head and buries himself in his military history books—hoping beyond hope that this time—one thing won't lead to another.

Superstock Dodge is windin' out in low
But my fuel injected Stingray's really startin' to go
To get the traction I'm ridin' the clutch
My pressure plate's burnin' that machines too much
Tach it up, tach it up, tach it up
Buddy, gonna shut you down
—The Beach Boys' "Shut Down," 1963

USA-1

A 1965 Corvette coupe barrels down the road. On the front, the car bears Chevrolet's classic advertising slogan "USA-1" license plate. (Photograph © Jerry Heasley)

Corvettes on the Silver Screen

Corvettes have appeared in many movies—some good, many bad. Yet whether most Corvette fans can remember the plot of those movies after all these years, they can almost certainly recall the year, model, and color of their favorite star.

Above:

Stingray

Stingray had it all: drug runners, machine gun-toting Playboy playmates, a spectacular car jump off St. Louis's Eads Bridge into the Big Muddy, and four red stunt Corvettes to be destroyed in high-speed hi-jinxes.

Right:

Corvette Summer

Sadly, 1978's Corvette Summer is probably the most famous 'Vette flick yet—sadly, because the movie and the starring Corvette leave much to be desired. Mark Hamill—long before he became Luke Skywalker—starred as a teenager in search of the thieves who stole his Corvette. He probably should have let them keep it.

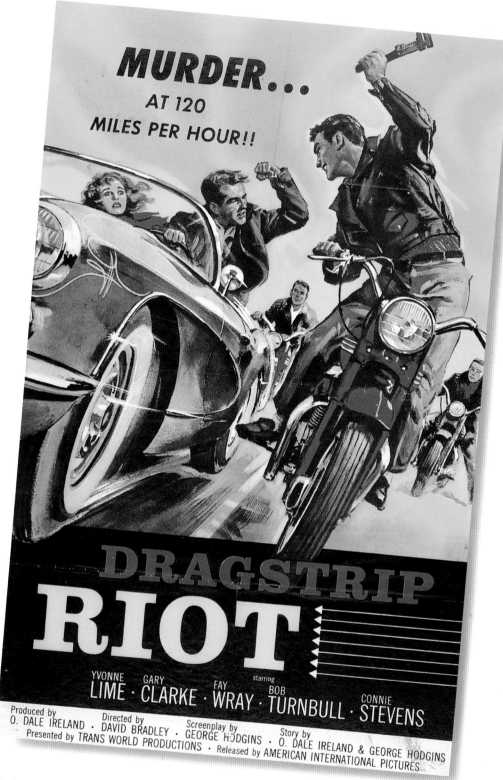

Dragstrip Riot

"Murder ... at 120 Miles Per Hour!!" promised this poster for 1958's Dragstrip Riot. *The flick featured hot rodders in a phalanx of Corvettes duking it out with bikers on Triumph twin motorcycles. Fay Wray of* King Kong *fame joined in the mêlée, which stopped only long enough for teen sensation Connie Stevens to sing a few rock'n'roll tunes.*

The Story of My Corvette

By John Wakefield

John Wakefield was bitten bad by the Corvette bug out of the blue one day. His saga to find his dream car is told here, but what he does not mention is that his white Corvette bears the license plate "AUTOBOT." The vanity plate name comes from his primary hobby of collecting toys from the 1970s, 1980s, and today, especially from the Transformers, from which the name Autobot is derived.

Facing page:

Bad Moon Rising

A 1998 C5 Corvette convertible takes on a new personality under a full moon. Convertibles had not been available since the last C4 of 1996, and their reappearance was welcomed by Corvettes fan everywhere. (Photograph © Jerry Heasley)

Inset:

2000 Corvette Flyer

Out of nowhere, early in January 1998, a switch clicked on in the back of my head and the notion was set in motion that I finally needed to put myself behind the wheel of a high-performance automobile.

Weeks of intense research afterward led me to the conclusion that the automobile of choice was the C5 Corvette, the latest generation of America's Sports Car. Previous generations of Corvette had not appealed to me all that much—save for the '63–'67 year models— but this latest iteration of the car was mind-blowingly inexpensive for the amount of performance it provided. And it looked pretty sharp, too.

Finding one with the option content I desired proved to be extremely difficult, however. My bottom line options: Arctic White exterior, Gray interior, six-speed manual tranny, and fog lamps. Finding one with the options I wanted *and* at a reasonable price was apparently damn-near impossible. I progressed to search around the nation for a C5 for about a month.

After hearing many different stories as to why no one could order me a new six-speed Vette, I ended up talking to Bill Heard Chevrolet in Huntsville, Alabama. They seemed to have a way around the various roadblocks in the ordering process and convinced me that they could get the car I was looking for.

So, on March 9, 1998, I placed my order for my white/gray coupe. For the next two months, I received constant assurances that the car would be built, despite the reported shortage of six-speed parts.

When word came back that my order had been canceled, I was upset. They tried to sell me a silver/ black six-speed coupe they had on the ground, but I rejected their offer and directed them to find a car exactly like or at least similar to what I had originally ordered.

A couple of days later, they called and said that they had found one at a dealership relatively close by, and asked me to come back in and talk it over. Their intention was to swap their silver/black car to the other dealer for this newfound white car and bring it back to Huntsville. I looked over the option list and they gave me their price. When I asked to go and see it before they had swapped it with the silver/black car, they balked big-time.

Displeased with their typical car-dealer shenanigans, I capitalized on a couple of crucial errors on their part that evening that pointed me in the right direction to exactly where the white car was: They should *never* have told me that it was "in a small town outside of Nashville," let alone left me by myself in their manager's office with all those phone numbers lying around!

I left the dealership telling them I would consider their offer and promptly went to work trying to locate the white car. After some good old-fashioned detective work, I finally was able to make a reasonable guess: Team Chevrolet in Smyrna, Tennessee. All I had to do now was call that dealership and see if my hunch was right or if I was going back to square one. By now, it was about midnight on Friday, May 8. The call would have to wait until morning.

The anxiety when I woke up Saturday morning was almost unbearable—much like it used to be on Christmas morning. There was another element in the air that morning, too. I would venture to call it an awareness that I was about to bear witness to and be part of a great historic event, one that would forever alter me and my perception of the world I live in.

I had called Team right as they opened, I think it was about 7:00. Speaking with a gentleman by the name of Bill Gilliam, I confirmed that they did indeed have the car that Bill Heard was trying to sell me, and that it was still available. They were a smalltown-sized dealership, and didn't get a large allocation of Corvettes. After hearing their initial asking price, I was dumbfounded, as it was not only below sticker price, but well below what Bill Heard's was asking. At that time, most dealers around the country were charging "sticker price *plus* $10,000" on all Corvettes. This price gouging has settled down quite a bit since then, but some dealers today are still doing this. And they wonder why they have trouble selling their 'Vettes. . . .

After this shock, I collected myself and told them I'd be there ASAP. Mr. Gilliam said they would have the car waiting out front for me when I arrived. I was in my Saturn and on the way there within a few minutes. There could have been three feet of snow on the ground, ice, tornadoes, hurricanes—it wouldn't have mattered. Nothing was going to stand in my way that morning.

I think I rolled onto their lot at about 9:30. When I pulled into the lot, the car was nowhere to be seen. I walked into the dealership to hunt for my salesman (who also thought the car should have been parked out front), and we went on a manhunt for the car. We walked around the front of the building, then down the length of the service area, all the way to the very back of the Team Chevy complex.

As I rounded the corner to the back of the building, a chill went through me. There it was, hiding away in the morning shade as if to say: "I ain't takin' no patients 'til that Wakefield fool gets here first!" As it turns out, the car had been on the ground for about a week or so.

When I sat behind the wheel, turned that key, and felt that Corvette grin creep across my face, I knew that if I left there that day without buying this car, I would regret it for the rest of my life.

So, on May 9, 1998, two months to the day after I had placed my initial order at Bill Heard, I bought my first Corvette at Team Chevrolet in Smyrna. Delivery was completed on May 13, 1998. It had most of the options I had originally ordered, and some I had not. Option content is as follows:

Job Number: 25594
Production (Build) Date: Monday, April 20, 1998
Item Description:
- AAB Memory Package
- AG2 ix-Way Power Passenger Seat
- B34 Front Floor Mats
- B84 Color Keyed Body Side Moldings
- C2L Roof Package (Coupe)
- CJ2 Dual Zone Electronic Air Conditioning
- D42 Luggage Shade and Parcel Net

- MN6 Six-Speed Manual Transmission
- T96 Fog Lamps
- UN0 Delco Bose Radio System
- Z51 Performance Handling Package

After application of discounts, rebates, and taxes, I saved about $2,300 buying the car at Team instead of through Bill Heard, proof positive that you *can* find a good deal on a new Corvette if you look hard enough. While I had not intended to get Z51 sport suspension and the in-dash CD, I realize now that these are indispensable options. To this day, I have still never sat in a car that so fit around me like a glove as does the C5. I consider myself beyond lucky to have found this car when I did. Some might call it destiny.

This is my first Corvette, and it definitely won't be my last. I can't say enough how awesome C5 is. I had initially planned to keep this car stock and original as possible. After an accident on the way up Monteagle Mountain resulted in replacing some body panels and repainting a good portion of the car, I'm having second thoughts about that. Over two and a half years after driving it off the lot in Smyrna, it's still too much fun to drive, and I continually find myself struggling to crank up my Saturn to go anywhere besides work.

A lot of the initial criticism I received right after I bought the car has long since abated. It takes some folks a while to come around, I guess. Choosing to become a Corvette owner remains a decision I'll never regret.

I was cruising in my Sting Ray late one night
When an XKE pulled up at the light
He rolled down the window of his shiny new Jag
And challenged me then and there to a drag
—Jan and Dean's "Dead Man's Curve," 1964

Overleaf:

Giant Dipper

With its fuel-injected 283-ci (4,636-cc) V-8 engine, the 1957 Corvette offered a thrill ride for its day equaled perhaps only by a rollercoaster. This '57 'Vette was a worthy alternative to the famous vintage wooden Giant Dipper rollercoaster on the boardwalk at Santa Cruz, California. (Photograph © Lucinda Lewis/All Rights Reserved)

The $200 '57 Fuelie

By Bob Antonick

The urban legend of the Corvette purchased for peanuts lives on in country music tunes, barroom boasts, and whispered stories between worshipful Corvette fans. Sometimes, the Corvette in question is the fabled diamond in the rust found

hidden beneath a haystack in a barn. Other times, it's the Corvette once owned by a baby-faced teenaged solider who was drafted away to Viet Nam never to return. And then there's the one that was sold by a jilted wife.

Here's one version of that famous urban legend, written as a tongue-in-cheek jest by Bob Antonick, the art director of *Corvette! The Sensuous American.*

Facing page:
The $200 '57 Fuelie
Red, red, and more red, from the dashboard to the steering wheel to the seat upholstery. They don't make them like this anymore. (Photograph © Jerry Heasley)

Inset:
1957 Corvette Operations Manual

*I*t was brand new. It glistened like polished pewter. The interior held the aroma of natural leather. Under its flowing lines murmured the promise of raw responsive power. It was Bill's new Corvette and he cherished it. Approvingly, he looked at it tucked safely away in his garage.

The weather was gray and laden with rain. The Corvette, Bill had decided, was never to be messed with polluted metropolitan air. Not while he had a say.

Bill's wife had other ideas.

"We need some milk." Joan pronounced one day. Bill squinted at the threatening weather.

"No way," Bill shook his head. "No way does that Corvette leave the garage if there's a chance of rain."

"It doesn't have to get wet," Joan said. "Take my car."

Bill glowered at the old humpback Buick Dynaflow that was carefully parked beside the drive. "You mean drive that thing all the way to the store?"

"Well, *I* drive it every day," Joan shrugged.

"You call that driving?" Bill asked. He had visions of his new Corvette safely ensconced in the garage, secure from those corrosive raindrops.

"Driving happens to be getting from point A to point B," Joan insisted. "Point B, in this case, is the grocery."

"Good point," Bill admitted cavalierly. "But I'm still not taking my Corvette out into that water wonderland."

"Great. Just great," Joan said. "We have an old clunker that can barely move, and a new car that you won't take out of the garage. Look, roadburner, we need some kind of basic transportation around here. Otherwise, we'll never get to the grocery. And if we don't get to the grocery, you don't eat."

Bill nodded slowly. Joan did have a way with words. He began scanning the classifieds. Somewhere, someone *had* to be selling a used car that wasn't too hateful. After a few days, he found a possible candidate. He scrutinized the ad, trying to find the ringer between the lines:

1957 CHEVY

NEEDS SOME WORK

MUST SELL

$200.00

The hooker was obviously in the second line.

"Needs some work" could mean anything from needing some rust scraped off to needing a new floorboard. Still, it was worth a try.

For two hundred bucks, the Chevy might be worth it even if the floorboards were falling out. Bill called the number and found it belonged to a law firm. The lawyer explained that the car was part of an estate that was being sold before the whole mess was sold at public auction and the lawyer might miss his normal settling fee.

Bill made an appointment to meet the lawyer at the estate the next day, confident that he just found a way to keep Joan happy.

Joan seemed less than thrilled the next morning when they woke to the sound of falling rain.

"I suppose this means you're taking the Buick."

"I don't want to look too prosperous by pulling up in the Corvette," Bill said.

"Still no milk," Joan grumbled and rolled over. "You'd better get yourself some breakfast while you're out," Joan said into the pillow.

If the day seemed damp and overcast, it was nothing compared to the lawyer. He made a Buffalo snowfall look like a sunny day. Bill decided that driving the Buick had been a smart move after he had seen the lawyer's sweaty palms.

"You the party interested in the used Chevy?" the lawyer asked quickly. Obviously, this was a man who could afford to waste no time. Time was money, y'know.

"Party of the first part," Bill grinned. The lawyer snorted his approval of Bill's attempt at humor.

"Car's in the garage."

"Let's take a look," Bill said resignedly. He was reminded of the old saying that lawyers had seven bodily openings. Aside from the normal six, they also had a special orifice that only accepted dollar bills.

They slogged around back and opened the garage. From the presents they had left behind, it was obvious that pigeons had been using the garage as a condominium for the past few years.

In the middle of the droppings was a low, cloth-covered shape.

Somehow, the contour did not look like any '57 Chevy Bill had ever seen in his life. It seemed too small. No fins.

"This the Chevy?" Bill asked.

A Long, Admiring Look

A 427-ci (6,994-cc) big-block under the bulging hood of your 1967 Corvette coupe was definitely worth a long, admiring look.

"That's it, all right," the lawyer agreed, pulling out a cigar. "You told me on the phone you were just looking for basic transportation, right?"

"Well, yes," Bill said, wondering just how basic Joan would be willing to consider.

"This is basic," the lawyer said, going through four matches to light the cigar.

"Sure seems low," Bill suggested.

"Been meaning to tell you about that," legal eagle said through a cloud of blue smoke. "I'm guessing the old man tried to do a little—what you call it?—customizing before he, uh, passed on."

"When was that?" Bill asked.

"'Bout fifteen years ago, give or take a few." The smoke was beginning to fill the garage.

Bill was feeling nauseous. "Tell me about this customizing."

"Maybe the old guy was trying to make a convertible," the lawyer hemmed. "Don't really know. But it looks like he cut the top off."

Great, Bill thought. Joan was really going to be happy.

The lawyer saw the expression on Bill's face. "Look, I don't want you to think I'm trying to pull anything. The title says '57 Chevrolet, and that's what it is.

Bill was ready to leave. "Let's take a quick look at the damage."

"Right." the lawyer wheezed. He yanked the filthy cloth back.

"Arg," Bill said. He was looking at a '57 Corvette roadster.

"Told you it was kinda messed up," the lawyer apologized.

"Man, you don't know," Bill gurgled.

"Two hundred bucks. Take it or leave it."

"Um, um, uh," Bill stuttered. Was it really possible that this shyster didn't know the difference between a '57 Chevrolet and a '57 Corvette? Should he tell the guy what was there under the dirty sheet?

"I can see it isn't quite what you expected," the lawyer said, chewing on his cigar. "You know I'm not trying to pull anything over on you. I told you the old man was probably trying to customize."

"Uh huh," Bill nodded.

"Did a pretty good job cutting the roof off, considering he was only a dentist," the lawyer mused. He bit off an end of the cigar and spat it out to join the pigeon droppings. "Guess he was handy with tools."

"Handy, yes," Bill said, forcing the tears out of his eyes.

"Look, I've got to unload this and clean up this estate. Tell you what. There's an old box over there. Maybe it has enough pieces in it to rebuild the roof. I'll toss that in for free.

"Pieces in a box," Bill repeated, still in shock. He decided he didn't want to upset the lawyer by telling him that the top was still on the car, folded in its compartment behind the seats. He followed the lawyer's glance to a cardboard box stained with old oil. "In that box?"

The lawyer shrugged. "Maybe it was a small roof."

"Yeah," Bill said. At the moment, he didn't care if the box held nothing but old crankcase oil. Gingerly, he toed it open. And almost strangled. He was looking at a factory-original '57 fuel injection system. "Jesus wept," Bill whispered.

The lawyer was looking over his shoulder. "Sure doesn't look like a roof. Guess the box was a little small, anyway."

"Can't keep a roof in there." Bill agreed.

"Bunch of old parts," the lawyer grumbled, chewing more actively on the cigar. "That old wreck probably needs all the help it can get, so I'll toss in those spare parts for free. Now that's fair."

Bill gurgled.

"Okay, so it isn't quite what you expected," the lawyer said, not realizing how true he was. "Tell you what I'm going to do just to prove I'm a nice guy. You buy this and I'll throw in the towing. Wherever you say. Now that's all fair, isn't it?"

Bill's head was beginning to clear. If he continued to sound reluctant, there was no telling what this greasy head would include. On the other hand, the next person to look at this "Chevy" might blab just what it was.

Bill held his breath. "Okay, I'll take it off your hands. Don't know what my wife will say, but okay."

"Man, you're a prince," the lawyer gushed. "You're really helping me out of a tight spot. To be honest, I didn't even look under that cloth. Many thanks, buddy."

"Oh, right," Bill said. He didn't bother to check the odometer, but the original Firestones still had plenty of rubber. He filled out the check and trundled home as quickly as the Buick could move, just beating the tow truck.

"What did you buy?" Joan asked suspiciously as Bill pulled his new Corvette out of the garage.

"A deal you won't believe," Bill said. He got his car out and wheeled in the '57. "This is going to be a restoration job the world has never seen. Heck, it hardly needs any work to begin with."

About an hour later, Joan came out to the garage to find Bill still staring at the '57 with great plans and dreams in his eyes.

"Hate to tell you this, hotshot," Joan said, "But we still need some milk."

"Sure, sure," Bill said, still dreamy-eyed. "Look, why don't you just take the Corvette down to the store."

"Your new Corvette? Are you positive?"

"Of course. The Buick is getting old. Probably old enough to be collectors' material," Bill smiled.

"Take your new Corvette?" Joan repeated incredulously.

"Not doing it any good sitting around. Sure, you can take it."

"Well, there's one little problem," Joan said quietly.

"What kind of problem? Buick in the way?"

"No," Joan said quietly. "I can't drive a stick-shift."

True story. Sort of. We have heard stories like this for years, from one end of the country to the other. Maybe there's some truth to it. We're not sure.

The details may vary, but the story is basically the same. The car may be stashed away in somebody's garage, or in a chicken coop, or behind the house.

The price changes, often in an inverse proportion to the value of the car. It may be only a hundred bucks, or two hundred, or four hundred. Rarely is the asking price more than a grand.

The Corvette itself changes. In one place, it may be a '54. In another place, it may be a fuel-injected '57.

The seller also changes. Sometimes it's a little old widow. Other times, it's a crusty old lawyer. Or a disgruntled divorcée. Old or young, it comes out the same.

For some strange reason, the buyer and the car have never been found. People we have talked to swear they know the guy, but he usually turns out to be the best friend of somebody's cousin. The car, if it can be seen at all, is conveniently just disappearing around the corner.

Maybe there's some truth to this story. Maybe the whole thing is pure fabrication. Either way, we would like to know for sure.

So we're asking for your help. If it is true, then someone made the Corvette buy of the century.

If you know the real buyer contact us. We want to talk to him or her. Especially, we want to photograph this world-shattering Corvette.

If you have a strong lead, contact us. Just give us a name and phone number.

If *you* are the lucky buyer, so much the better.

One way or the other, we will make it worth your while. So tell us.

But please. Just the facts.

A body like yours oughta be in jail
Cuz it's on the verge of bein' obscene
Move over, baby, gimme the keys
I'm gonna try 2 tame your little red love machine
—Prince's "Little Red Corvette," 1983

CHAPTER 4

The Need for Speed

"Sunset Strip"
A Corvette faces off against its early days arch-rival, the Ford Thunderbird, in this painting by Dave Barnhouse. (Original art by Dave Barnhouse © 2002 Hadley Licensing, Bloomington, MN)

☆ ☆ ☆

Fate, Speeding, Music, the Open Road, and My 1961 Corvette

By Chaz Cone

Chaz Cone first fell in love with Corvettes when he was fourteen and ran across a photograph of the first 1953 model in a magazine. Since then, he has owned a variety of Corvettes of various vintages, but that first image still burns in his mind.

When he got his first Corvette, Chaz naturally had to take it on the road. The story of that road trip is a picaresque adventure, a classic among Corvette tales.

Facing page:
"Splitting Image"
Artist Scott Jacobs's image of a 1963 Corvette split-window coupe captures one of the car's most distinctive angles. (Artwork © 2002 by Scott Jacobs/Segal Fine Art)

Inset:
1961 Corvette Brochure

The Setup

I am old. Well, by some standards, I'm "middle aged" (whatever that is), but when cops look to you like they're teenagers, I think you've crossed some sort of line. Men my age (and younger) face their "mid-life crisis" in various ways. I wanted a mid-life crisis, but my wife wouldn't let me have one.

Sigh.

So I don't call the recent acquisition of my 1998 Black/Light Oak Automatic Targa convincing evidence of a mid-life crisis (*pshaw!*), and I can prove it. See, I also have a 1990 Red/Red/White Roadster (now *that* possibly *was* a mid-life crisis). My wife won't let me

sell it. Her reasoning: Every two-person family needs at least two Corvettes; the red one is "hers." So, "we" have two Corvettes. Sounds right to me.

Anyhow, the subject of this story is my Corvette experience of nearly forty years ago.

The Buildup

It was 1961. I was a wet-behind-the-ears graduate from Georgia Tech, driving my first Corvette, a cherry 1960 Silver/White cove, removable hardtop, three-speed manual (it was bought used but I *did* have indulgent parents). I was lucky enough to get hired by IBM in Atlanta the day after graduation and was transferred

(overnight—what a surprise!) to the IBM office in Greenville, South Carolina. I don't want to insult Greenvillians (is that a word?) but the culture shock of moving from Atlanta (yay!) to Greenville (boo!) must have seriously affected my young mind.

There I was, single, in a small town with a cool car, no debt, and a new job paying the princely sum of (get this!) $6,000 per year. That was so much money in 1961 that I had to bail out my checking account every week or so to keep it from overflowing. Truly. I *had* to do something to dispose of some of that money....

So, I went to Mike Persia Chevrolet in Greenville and traded my perfectly good 1960 Vette in on a brand

new '61 Honduras Maroon/Black, removable hardtop, four-speed. Yep, I traded in the car just to get another gear in the shifter. Ah, the folly of youth.... But this car was much faster than the '60—either that, or I learned how to shift faster.

OK. So it got to be November 1961 and time for Homecoming Weekend at Georgia Tech. Hey, I'm a big-shot college graduate with a brand-new Corvette (and a girlfriend at Emory University in Atlanta), so I headed to Atlanta to snow the underclassmen—and the girl. A fine time was had by all.

A very fine time.

It's now midnight, Sunday. Tech beat the Duke Blue Devils, and it's time to go home. I have to be at work at 8:30 in the morning and (at that time) it took three hours to drive back to Greenville. It was a beautiful clear night. I mean "clear."

Very clear.

Very.

This was just barely before the interstate highway system was built. The road then from Atlanta to Greenville was U.S. 29, two-lane blacktop. I was heading north, and the moon was full. The night was cold and crisp, and the visibility was unlimited. I was happy. I was going fast.

Very fast.

Very, very fast.

It was glorious. Just glorious.

The moonlight was bright, but not quite so bright as the red-and-blue flasher I noticed in my rearview: Two Georgia state troopers. They were exceedingly polite and quite impressed with my car. I thought for a while that we'd just have a nice 1:15 A.M. chat on the side of the road and that I'd be allowed to go on my way. Well, I was young and naïve.

They thought it better that I follow them into Carnesville, Georgia—just a few miles back down the road toward Atlanta—and meet the local sheriff. No problem. And I had no trouble following them; they weren't going all that fast.

We reached Carnesville in due course, and they accompanied me to the front door of a small house on the town square and rang the doorbell. It was five min-

Wide Body
This wide-body 1978 modified Corvette coupe is dressed in bodywork crafted by John Greenwood based on his years designing race cars. (Photograph © Jerry Heasley)

utes before the door was opened by a giant in a night-shirt. Imagine a really tall Charlie Daniels look-alike in a full-length nightshirt—with his badge pinned to his chest. Apparently being awakened in the middle of the night by the State Patrol was routine for the Sheriff. He directed us to the basement entrance and said he'd meet us there. We walked down and around to the back of the house, and the Sheriff met us at an outside door. We (the Sheriff and I) bid goodnight to the two troopers and they drove away. And left me there. With the man-mountain.

He turned out to be a cordial man. We sat down in his basement office, which was pretty much like the one in the old *Andy Griffith Show*. There were two empty jail cells (doors open) on the far wall. We had a nice chat.

Sheriff: "Well, son, the troopers clocked you at 95 in a 50 zone. Does that sound about right?"

Chaz: "If that's what they said, sir, I guess it's true."

Sheriff: "The fine for 45 mph over the limit is $90. Just pay the fine and you're free to go."

Chaz: "Sheriff, I'd be happy to pay that fine, but I've been in Atlanta all weekend and all the cash I have is $15. But I'd be happy to write you a check."

Sheriff: "Son, this is a small town but I'm not a fool. It's cash on the barrel-head or you can spend the night here in my jail."

Chaz: "But if I stay here I won't have the money in the morning, either. Isn't there another way?"

Sheriff: "Well, you could call your boss and have him bring the money down."

Chaz: "I just reported for work in Greenville a few weeks ago. I don't think my career would survive waking up an IBM branch manager in the middle of the night to drive the money for a speeding-ticket fine down to Carnesville."

Sheriff: "I can understand that. Tell you what: Why don't you leave your spare tire here so I can be sure you'll come back with the fine?"

Chaz: "Sheriff, I really appreciate that. But the way my luck's running I'd get ten miles out of town, have a flat, and spend the night on the side of the road. But I'll tell you what I can do. In my car I have a Gibson flattop guitar worth more than $300. Suppose I leave it here and come back next week to pay the fine?"

Sheriff: "Go get it, son."

I was back in a flash with my guitar.

Sheriff: "You play that?"

I rejected my first three wise-ass answers.

Chaz: "I play a little."

Sheriff: "Play me somethin'."

Chaz: "It's almost two o'clock in the morning!"

Sheriff: Play me somethin'."

So I sat down on the bunk in one of the cells and played a few folk songs (remember this was 1961). So help me, he went upstairs, woke his wife and two small sons, and I sat there and played Kingston Trio songs for a half-hour. Little boys about four and six. All four of them just sittin' and listenin' while I was pickin' and a-grinnin'.

Eventually they let me stop. We put the guitar into its case, put the case on the bunk, and he locked it up (clang!). I got into my car and drove (observing the speed limit carefully) back to Greenville and fell into bed.

The Payoff

Fast-forward forty-eight hours to Tuesday afternoon. After work I went to the bank and got $90 in cash and headed on down to Carnesville just as it began to get dark. Remember now, I was on my way to pay a speeding ticket. Would *anyone* speed under those circumstances? No, and neither would I. I was driving south on U.S. 29 at a sedate 55 mph.

As I approached the Georgia state line, I noticed a sign that said "Interstate Highway 85 Open." Wow! I can get to Carnesville and back much faster!

I got onto the new interstate. It was beautiful, four lanes as far as the eye could see with a nice median. But I set the speedometer carefully on the double-nickel, and it was a great road. I noticed that there wasn't any signage yet, and there weren't any lines painted but it was a full moon (remember that!) and visibility was great.

Great, that is, until I topped a little rise (going just 55 mph) and found that I-85 ended, and there was a ninety-degree cut to the left back to U.S. 29. Seems that they hadn't yet gotten around to building the bridge over Lake Hartwell.

I spun the wheel and braked and downshifted furiously and succeeded in getting the Vette turned a few degrees to the left—and then we went down a twenty-foot embankment into Lake Hartwell. I remember thinking that Corvettes, being plastic, might float.

Sigh.

The only thing keeping me from converting the

Vette into a fiberglass inboard runabout was a stump in the water about a foot below the surface. We struck it and stopped immediately. I mean *immediately!* My glasses flew off and broke the windshield but I was securely belted in and wasn't injured (the luck of the stupid, I guess). The car was sitting in about two feet of water and the water was, therefore, about halfway up the side.

I opened the door a little. Water came in, so I closed it again.

I was sitting there dazed and pissed off, and then I noticed a revolving red-and-blue light up on the road behind me. No, it was a different policeman; this time, a South Carolina state trooper. He got out of his car, cupped his hands around his mouth, and shouted, "Run off the road?"

I rejected the first half-dozen wise-ass remarks (I was getting good at suppressing wise-ass remarks) and yelled back, "Yes, sir!"

He walked a rope down and tied it (I learned later) to some fragile part of my rear suspension. (Note: Hauling a Corvette around by a rope tied to a sensitive rear-suspension component is not a good idea. Not at all.)

He used his prowler to pull us (me and the Corvette) back up onto the road. A cursory inspection showed cracks in both front fenders and a smashed area below the grill. But the car started (hallelujah!). The trooper told me that I was the third one that day. Later—much later—I tried to get some relief from the Department of Transportation, the contractors, the state of South Carolina, and the State of Georgia for opening a road with no signage and no barrier to a lake entry by car, but to no avail.

I thanked the trooper and limped on down to Carnesville. I visited the Sheriff, showed him the damage (a lot of *tsk, tsk*-ing), paid the fine, recovered my guitar, and started back to Greenville. The suspension felt funny but I was able to make it all the way back home.

Here's a little-known fact: Mike Persia Chevrolet (in those days) had a service department that was open twenty-four hours a day. I drove the car down a ramp and into the service bay and turned it over to a service writer. I didn't get the car back for nine weeks! That's how long it took in those days to get all the plastic forward of the windshield from St. Louis where Corvettes were built at the time. The transmission was never quite right after that and—and here's the sad part—I decided to get married while the car was in the shop.

My new bride, who drove a Sunbeam Alpine, reasoned that we didn't need two sports cars and that I, of course, would be the one to give up his. I should have known the marriage wouldn't work. So at the age of twenty-two, I was married and Corvette-less.

When the marriage ended two years later, I was the one blessed to receive the Sunbeam Alpine in the settlement. I drove that car directly to the nearest Chevy dealer in Atlanta (I'd been transferred back) and traded it in on a brand-new Yellow/Black/Black '65 four-speed roadster. And later, the '65 went for an exact-same-color '67. Which we (new wife, now) kept for fourteen years. When I sold it (for more than I'd paid for it) I actually cried as the guy drove it away.

It only took twelve more years before I got our '90 Red roadster and eight more years until the '98 Black Targa and now only six months until my new '64 roadster. Quite a saga. And, before I die, I plan to have a '60, a '61, a '65, and a '67 again.

Seems only right.

Little red Corvette
Baby you're much 2 fast . . .
—Prince's "Little Red Corvette," 1983

THE GLEN NATIONALS

A weekend of the finest amateur road racing in this country ... one of twelve North American "SuperNationals" awarding extra points to competitors toward season ending National Championships in 24 Sports Car Club of America competition classes ... the spectrum of road racing machinery -- from McLarens and Corvettes to Formula Vee and Showroom Stock ... more than 250 entries expected for the oldest sports car road races in this country ... for the spectator, a weekend of spacious camping areas and rolling meadows for picnicking ... bring the hibachi and the family for a weekend of "super" National road racing competition ...

WATKINS GLEN, N.Y.

SCHEDULE: Practice and qualifying for all cars Friday from 1 - 5 p.m.; Practice and qualifying Saturday until 3 p.m., first three 14 lap sprint races. Sunday, beginning 1:05 p.m., final four 14 lap sprint races.

AUG. 11-12-13

-- TICKETS: WEEKEND $10; SUNDAY ONLY $5; PADDOCK & GARAGE PASS $5 --

FREE SEATS   TOYOTA PACES THE RACES   FREE CAMPING

☆ ☆ ☆

The Corvette Racer: A Sprite Driver's View, From a Safe Distance

By Peter Egan

Peter Egan has become a sort of garage prophet of car buffs and motorcyclists. He is equal parts sage and common man, imparting wisdom from the school of hard knocks and relating tales of car and motorcycling culture chock full of universal truths.

Peter wrote this fun article for *Road & Track* in the 1970s. In fact, it was so much fun that the magazine's editor-in-chief, John Dinkel, suggested Peter continue on this tack and create a regular monthly column. The rest is history.

Facing page:

Make Way for Corvettes

This late 1960s race poster announced The Glen Nationals at Watkins Glen, New York.

Inset:

2001 Corvette C5-R Flyer

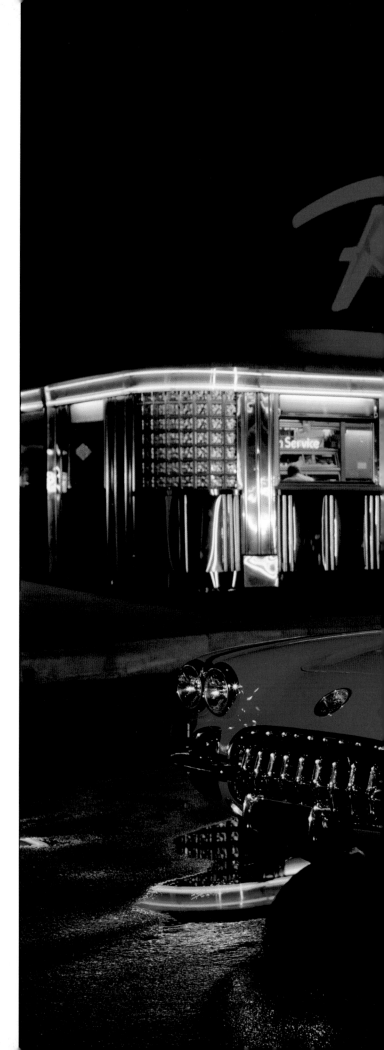

To those of us who raced our diminutive H Production Sprites and similarly high-pitched cars in Midwest Council and SCCA regionals, Corvette drivers were always a breed apart. We spent many weekends pitted next to Corvette teams, adjusting our pathetic tiny Austin valves or performing some other jeweler's chore on our Bugeyes, watching these fiberglass behemoths and the crews who serviced them out of the corner of one collective eye (we didn't have the nerve to stare with both eyes). Corvette drivers and Sprite drivers didn't mix much, except to borrow the occasional strand of safety wire or half roll of duct tape from one another, but a shortage of information and personal contact didn't prevent us from forming some well developed stereotypes and generalizations.

We knew a few things about Corvette guys:

Corvettes always seemed to he raced by drivers who had crew cuts long after everyone else in the club looked like George Harrison. You got the feeling that if they weren't driving Corvettes, they'd he dropping you for fifty pushups at Camp Lejeune or chewing Copenhagen without taking it out of the can. Corvette guys drove in black Wellington boots while everyone else wore effete moccasins or Nomex booties. They wore open-face helmets with no visors so everyone could see them scowl. When they dressed up to go out at night they wore white nylon windbreakers, white pants, Goodyear caps with the visors pulled down over the eyes, and at least one article of clothing with stars and stripes or crossed checkered flags on it, and they always went out for pizza and beer in a place with bright neon lights.

Corvette drivers adjusted their points with air wrenches and their pit men were sometimes crushed to death by fallen lug nuts. Corvette guys had trailers with six wheels and towed them with brand-new extended-cab white pickup trucks with more checkered flags and stars and stripes on them. The trailers had

Rosie's Diner

A 1960 Corvette convertible shares the parking lot with a bevy of classic cars at Rosie's Diner in Rockford, Michigan, on Highway M-57. Rosie's was a prefabricated diner with the signature stainless-steel exterior made by the venerable Paramount Dining Company of Oakland, New Jersey, in 1945. Since its opening that year, the diner has served up millions of dinners, followed by a slice of Rosie's famous homemade pie. (Photograph © Lucinda Lewis/All Rights Reserved)

Speedster

Reeves Callaway's limited run of Corvette Speedsters were inspired by the classic American speedsters from Auburn, Stutz, and Mercer as well as by the Bonneville Salt Flats recordsetters. Callaway Advanced Technology built just ten Series I Speedsters in 1991 with the L-98 twin turbo. The Series II Speedsters, like this car, were launched in 1992 powered by the SuperNatural LT5 with 490 hp. (Photograph © Jerry Heasley)

overhead tire racks with tires that were exactly four times as wide as they were tall. These tires cost $600 a piece and lasted only one practice session before being torn to bits by raw torque.

Corvette drivers never asked any questions at drivers' meetings.

When a Corvette driver started his engine the smoke and noise came out of side pipes the size of storm sewers, and the exhaust pulses threw large chunks of gravel and blew your tent down. When these engines blew up on the track, the concussion and coolant spray left corner workers dripping and dazed for hours.

If a Corvette threw a rod through its sump, the resulting oil spill made your Sprite go backwards through Turn 3 for the rest of the season.

Every Corvette driver had at least one gold tooth. Corvette drivers made their money in cattle or lumber, or else they owned more than one gas station and paid men named Frank to run it for them. Corvette drivers themselves had names like Bart or Chuck or Bob, and their last names were usually Johnson. They always had Texas jet pilot accents even if they were from Michigan's Upper Peninsula.

Corvette drivers used hacksaws to set their camber and had tool chests where each tool occupied a whole drawer. The sockets at the small end of their socket sets started at 1¼ in. and went upward to sizes that frightened Caterpillar mechanics. Between races, Corvette drivers arcwelded things to their chassis in a blinding shower of sparks. When a Corvette driver jacked up his car, he didn't so much lift the car, as push the earth away from it.

Male Corvette drivers had blonde wives who chainsmoked and had cattle ranch tans and pale blue eyes, while women Corvette drivers were always single because they couldn't find anyone who was man enough to marry them. Corvette drivers never lit their cigars. They just chewed them flat and walked around the pits until they saw the front suspension on a Lotus Seven or the engine in a Sprite. Then they threw the flat, wet cigars on the ground in disgust.

Corvette drivers used approximately 100 gallons of Union 76 racing gas on every lap and had government surplus fuel cells from armored vehicles. While those of us in Sprites, Midgets, and Spitfires had to *drive* from one end of the main straight to another, Corvette drivers simply *launched* themselves in a great belch of power and landed at the other end on four smoking tires. Corvette drivers drove on a much shorter track than we did, and their pitboards flew by like fastballs and were impossible for the human eye to read, while we had time to examine the small print on the race marshal's badge-littered vest.

When Corvette drivers massed on the starting grid for the A and B Production races at Elkhart Lake, the announcer used to say, "Ladies and Gentlemen, it's time to shake the dew off the lilies." He didn't say that before the other races, because nothing else thundered, rumbled, and shook the ground quite the same way.

Not even Sprites.

Automobile Magazines Past and Present

The covers of our favorite automobile magazines present a history of the Corvette through their images and stylings. Here is a sampling of Corvette covers from the beginning, showing the way we were.

Road & Track *December 1957*

Above:
Road & Track *June 1954*

Right:
Sports Car World *August 1964*

SOLID AXLE RACING CAR-A NEW DESIGN

CAR LIFE

50 CENTS
NOVEMBER 1967

TESTING: A PAIR OF GERMAN
GRAND TOURING MACHINES
BMW CS 2000 COUPE
BMW R69S CYCLE
AND, THE 1968 RIVIERA

CORVETTES
From 1954 to 1968
the history, the cult & a tech analysis

COMPARING THE LUXURY THREE

"KNOW YOUR CAR"
A new pictorial series
JULY 1960 35¢

MOTOR TREND

CORVETTE – The Best One Yet?

GM's New Bubble-Top Bomb

LOOK WHAT'S COMING FOR '67!

AUGUST 1966   60¢ IN CANADA   FIFTY CENTS

CAR LIFE

COOL OFF WITH AIR CONDITIONING

ROAD TESTS
OLDSMOBILE 442
CADILLAC CALAIS
PONTIAC SPRINT

CORVETTES for the Go·Go Set
427/4·speed and 327/automatic

Above, left:
Car Life *November 1967*

Above, right:
Motor Trend *July 1960*

Left:
Car Life *August 1966*

The Fastest Corvettes
I Have Known

By Jerry Heasley

Jerry Heasley is the Ansel Adams of the Corvette. Over his decades as a magazine and book photographer, he has probably photographed more Corvettes than most fans have even seen.

Jerry has also written about Corvettes for numerous magazines and books. Some were stock cars, others racers, and still others modifieds. Asked to pull together a gallery of the fastest Corvettes he has known, he presented these six machines spanning the Corvette's history from the C1 to the C5.

Facing page:
Rocket Roadster
This modified 1954 Corvette retains the spirit of the original but is enhanced in its styling with modern mechanicals and the best of the best in bodywork and detailing. (Photograph © Jerry Heasley)

Inset:
1994 Corvette Brochure

Wretched Excess

Rich Rimbold can talk the talk and walk the walk. Who couldn't once they've gone to such great lengths of excess? Actually, Rich, who is a college professor, has gone a step past excess to what he labels "wretched excess," followed by one giant stage of performance he calls, "You've got to be kidding."

His '98 C5 is currently the one and only twin-turbo 427 wide body in the world. With 725 horsepower, of which 613, along with 679 foot pounds of torque, transfer to the rear wheels, Rich's ride is, as he says, "In league with the likes of a McLaren F1."

For the uninformed, the McLaren center-seat exotic sells for over a million dollars, which puts in sharp perspective the "hundred and a half" Rimbold spent on his Lingenfelter.

Initially, Rich merely wanted his Corvette modified by Lingenfelter. He sent his 'Vette to Lingenfelter Performance Engineering for installation of a Stage 1 twin turbo on his stock LS1 motor. Today, Rimbold is a trifle blasé with his recollection of 500 horsepower. "We started showing the car at various concourse events. We also enjoyed it out on the highway."

A year later, Rich went back to Lingenfelter to upgrade to the 383 stroker, still with twin turbos. To intellectualize his reasoning, the associate provost at Coppin State College and law professor at the prestigious Johns Hopkins University in Baltimore, offered, "There is a kind of excess and a wretched excess."

"Wretched excess" may be described as that state of tune in which performance has advanced so far as to be pitiful, forlorn, despicable. In street lingo, car people have just used the word "bad." College professors can be more articulate. Another comparable term would be "filthy rich." Why do you need another billion dollars, you ask Bill Gates. Or, to use a cliché, why do you climb that mountain? In Rich Rimbold's world, wretched excess was not a limit. He wanted more power. He got *badder*.

At the same time as the 383 stroker came the Bad Ass look, the glorious wide body, developed by Lingenfelter for post-200-mph testing. Rimbold heard the tale from the source.

"I think that is part of the reason LPE designed the body. After John Lingenfelter turned that 225 or 226 in his Stage II twin turbo, it was kind of a little light. So the body may have been in response to meeting the needs for high-speed stability."

In a manner of speaking, the C5 body was "too aerodynamic." What was needed was more downforce and thus more drag, more stability to hold the road. A side benefit of the wide body is the ability to carry a wider set of wheels and tires.

If Rimbold had made a hit with his twin-turbo C5 stock-bodied coupe, he became the darling of concourse showing in his *Wretched Excess* clothes. He placed second in the entire East Region in concourse events. But alas, poor wide body, stone chips from highway cruising had taken their points toll. Rich sent the 'Vette back to LPE for paint.

Rimbold was not one to pass up opportunity. He shipped the C5 from Maryland to Indiana. The 427 was a possibility. LPE explained the C5 R block was available. Rich gave the okay, "Let's do it."

The result is the first 427 twin turbo installed in the wide body, creating the "You've got to be kidding" 'Vette. The combination begs we answer the two questions kids and adults alike pose on feasting their eyes upon this creation. Already, we have hinted at the answer to "how much," which is "a hundred and a half." But, how fast is she?

Rich makes it clear he is a responsible driver and does not have the skills to take this car to its limits, either in the quarter mile or top speed. Off the bat we'll say 0–60 mph in 2.97. With the beefed-up automatic, all you got to do is aim, floor the pedal, and hang on. One thousand one, one thousand two, one thousand three, end of story.

For the quarter, Rich looks to another 427 twin-turbo LPE drivetrain, also automatic, just like his, but without the wide body. In the hardtop, this LPE-built car ran a 9.36 @ 151.7.

As for top speed, according to Rich, "They have estimated the top speed at over 240 mph."

Rimbold also gave us a peek inside LPE. "I was told by the folks at Lingenfelter that they have something known as Project 255. The old Sledgehammer Corvette turned a closed-course speed record at 254.7. That's probably the reason for 255."

We get it. As for the tune of the particular car, Rich does not know. However, he has offered his silver wide body.

For now, Rich and his wife are content to show their awesome 'Vette and to occasionally "fracture" the speed limit. Cars this fast don't just break the limits.

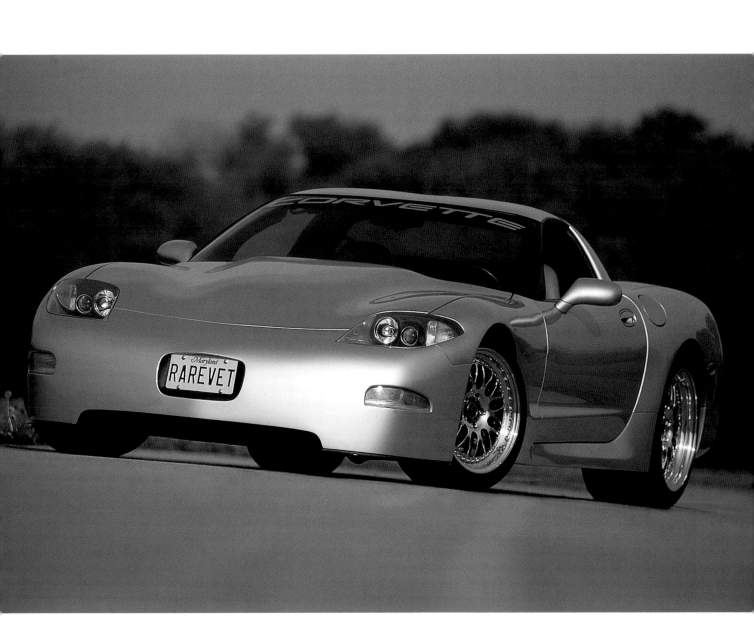

Wretched Excess

The C5 never looked faster. This 1998 C5 is the world's only twin-turbo 427-ci (6,994-cc) wide body, with thanks to Lingenfelter Performance Engineering. With 725 hp under the hood, it's in a league with McLaren's F1 supercar. (Photograph © Jerry Heasley)

Talmage-Mobile C5

Talmage Dobbs sounds like the name of a Southerner who writes Civil War history books and likes to toss back a couple of drinks with his shrimp on the barbie. Two out of three isn't too bad of a guess; Talmage doesn't write.

What he does do best is race, and we don't mean in and out of corners. "I'm an expert drag racer," Talmage says, then admits he wasn't so expert handling the twin turbo.

The fifty-nine-year-old, fun-loving thrill-seeker has a couple of neat toys—this normally aspirated C5, a 383 Lingenfelter tuner 2000 coupe, and a twin turbo mate with a Caravaggio interior he calls his "Goochie Mobile." See why we fancy him a Southern writer?

Actually, Talmage tells a good tale. Here's one he spun, which is true and not for a fiction book. Dobbs journeyed to Canada for a speedometer reading 0 to 300 to fit in his 2000 'Vette. In an indignant, friendly tone, he says, "Yes, I paid $800 to get it. I took the car to Toronto. I had to sign all this paperwork, and GM said 'What in God's name does a man in Atlanta, Georgia, want the Canadian cluster for?' And John Lingenfelter said 'Well, he likes to tease bimbos.'"

Actually, no more proper Southern gentleman ever walked into a 'Vette show or drag race. Talmage is apt to get plenty of attention when he does. His 'Vettes turn heads, like this 383 Lingenfelter. In Talmage's concise verbiage, "I wanted him to put the 383 in it with headers and make it go fast. And he did."

After the tuner work, Talmage installed headlights and foglights from Breathless Performance. "They are a copy of lights in the #2 C5-R that won the 24 Hours of Daytona. They are awesome. I like the plastic covers. They don't flip up and down."

Next, Talmage sent his 2000 coupe to Caravaggio Corvettes in Canada for installation of the red-and-black interior. "I get criticized all the time for spending

Talmage-Mobile C5
This 2000 C5 ups the ante with a 383-ci (6,274-cc) Lingenfelter twin-turbo engine. The red-and-black interior was courtesy of Caravaggio Corvettes, and the Breathless Performance headlights and foglights are copies of lights from the C5-R. (Photograph © Jerry Heasley)

$10,000 for my interior. They call me a fool." John's response is poetic, "Well, hell."

The interior is incredible. Talmage is so impressed with Caravaggio's work he says, "If something isn't perfect, it does not go out of there. It is going to be perfect."

Paying homage to Caravaggio's artistic talents, he let us know, "I've spent time with Caravaggio. There was an Italian artist. I mean a dead artist right now, but his name was Caravaggio. And John has his book, and I looked at it. It is like Matisse or something."

Talmage ran his 383 Lingenfelter and the Goochie Mobile through the quarter mile at Beech Bend Raceway Park in Bowling Green, Kentucky. The 475-horsepower 383 ran consistent 11.4s. The twin-turbo 350, boasting 500 horsepower, ran a best ET of 11.8 in three runs. "You need more technique with the twin turbo," Talmage told us. "And since that was the first day I drove the car, I felt very, very nervous. Finally, I turned the car over to John Lingenfelter himself. He got it down to 11.4."

Both cars ran street tires. Obviously, the twin turbo could have used racing slicks, but the horsepower advantage at 500 was not overwhelming either. Talmage tells this story to illustrate how great an all-around car the Lingenfelter 383 is. The vehicle utilizes the street tires to the max.

Dobbs kept the stock suspension, which he ordered with the Z51 Performance Handling package and JL4 Active Handling System. He replaced the stock 17-inch wheels with BBS of the same size. "I just like to be different," Talmage offered. "It could be a birth defect."

Z07

There are tuners and then there are tweakers. Sriyantha Weerasuria of Elite Motorsports in Austin, Texas, considers himself the latter. He's actually more. MTI in Houston did build his motor and modified the drivetrain on his hardtop. Sriyantha, who friends call SW, did the rest.

His goal was to build the fastest six-speed C5. "I set my mind to have the fastest C5 around, the fastest six-speed car. You could make an automatic run faster, but a six-speed takes a little bit more driving skill."

SW, in typical form, is being modest. Turning a 9.98 second ET, he shifts gears at about 6,300 rpm. With the TNT nitrous engaged (135-horse shot) all the way down the strip, he stabs the clutch and grabs gears with the shortened throw shifter, ending up in fourth through the traps at a phenomenal 145.2 mph.

Yet, take a look at his black-on-black C5, inside and out. You find a clean-as-a-whistle, GT-type 'Vette, RK Sport elevated hood, body lowered a couple inches, riding on 18-inch Fiske wheels, and looking ready for a trip to the local country club. "Wet Oakley" seat covers keep him from sliding on the stock leather. The air blows cold, yet there is a noticeable radicalness to the cam timing. Obviously, SW's C5 is far from stock.

The major curiosity for most onlookers is the set of front fender badges. "Everybody knows the Z06," SW smiles. "They're just trying to figure out what a Z07 is."

This C5 is a '99, or two years prior to the Z06. The starting point for the engine build was the LS1, which is MTI's specialty today. When they bored and stroked the motor to 422 cubes—about 7 liters—and used many Z06 parts, including LS6 intake and heads, the Z07 moniker made a lot of sense.

One shouldn't ask MTI for an identical Z07 build. "It's kind of a one-off motor. I'm like their test bed," SW says.

His need for speed pushed the Z07 concept past boundaries. SW reveals, "Every time we modified something, we created a new problem. We were experimenting a lot."

One example is the solid roller cam, a custom grind that SW and MTI are keeping secret for now. "With the solid roller, we had problems with the lifters making noise. We'd adjust them, run the car for about an hour, and they started backing off. We had to buy the same race setup as the C5-R. The lifters alone cost $2,000. You adjust them and you are done. It's almost like hydraulics. We've only adjusted them once."

SW and MTI didn't bolt all the parts and pieces together, then go to the strip and turn a 9.99. Making Z07 perform was a learning curve. With 620 horsepower at the flywheel and close to 800 with the nitrous shot, Z07 is a test car.

"I had some problems at the beginning. The car didn't want to shift good. We had to do a lot. We went back and forth and got the McCloud dual disc clutch shimmed where the car would shift."

The learning curve continued at the strip. "You've got to be able to launch correctly. I've broken an inner

Z07

The Z06 C5 didn't make its debut until 2001, but this 1999 coupe was retrofitted with an LS1 engine that was bored and stroked to 422 ci (6,912 cc) and topped off with numerous Z06 parts, including LS6 intake and cylinder heads. Add a shot of nitrous oxide, and the Z07 moniker makes perfect sense. (Photograph © Jerry Heasley)

stub axle. I've broken a clutch. I've twisted the long in-put shaft from the back of the motor to the transmission."

SW's first runs at the strip were 10.3, 10.2 10.3, at 143–144 mph. He admits, "It took me quite a while to get into the high 9s. I went from 10.2 to a 10.15, then a 10.09."

The secret is proper launch. "When I ran my first ET in the 9s, a 9.99 @ 144, I had a 1.48-second sixty-foot time. And that's pretty good with an IRS."

He discovered leaving the line at less rpm—3,000 instead of 4,500—yielded slower sixty-foot times but a quicker ET. His latest foray into the 9s was a 9.98 @ 145.2 mph. On this run, he had a 1.55-second sixty-foot time. "I didn't feel like I was hurting the car at all when I left."

SW's Z07 has no roll cage. His original goal wasn't to build a drag car, but the Z07 is streetable. It doesn't overheat. The air blows cold. He can drive it anywhere.

SW's tweaking continues. His Z07 should get faster. He has decided to install a six-point roll cage so he can compete in more events. He'll up the nitrous boost to a 200-horse shot, which is going to require a bigger fuel system. On the test dyno, SW has found out the air/

fuel ratios are already on the lean side. He says with amazement, "I'm running the same fuel pump and fuel lines rated for the 345-horsepower LS1."

One has to wonder. Is this the fastest street C5 in the world? SW says, "So far that I know of anywhere in the world, this is the fastest six-speed C5."

He could be right. There are tuners and then there are tweakers. SW is the latter.

King of the Hill

"When the boost comes on, all hell breaks loose. It feels like you've been shot out of a damn cannon," Paul Dehnert says of his ZR1 twin turbo. With 850 horsepower at the flywheel and 742 pound-feet of torque delivered to the rear wheels, we are not surprised.

The ZR1, apparently, is king of the hill of C4 tuner Corvettes, at least of the street breed. Dehnert could not think of a more powerful 'Vette with such a docile nature in traffic. "I'm sure there are more powerful race cars. But, this ZR1 is designed to run on the street with the AC turned on and all the creature comforts of a stock ZR1. I mean, that car will idle around town. I could send my wife down to the grocery store for a quart of milk—or I should say she could send me down—and it runs just like a stock ZR1. That's how docile it is when it is not on the boost."

About a year and a half ago, Dehnert took his low-mileage ZR1 to Lingenfelter to install a twin turbo. Paul has always favored the LT5 DOHC engine. "The thing I like about the ZR1 is the engineering uniqueness, the fact it is a DOHC, Lotus-designed engine, built by Mercury Marine. The engineering is phenomenal."

Dehnert also knew GM built a twin turbo LT5; there is one on display at the National Corvette Museum. GM's version of the twin-turbo made 650 horses.

Paul wondered what John Lingenfelter could do with such a build. John was pretty interested to tackle the project, too. Dehnert got together with another ZR1

King of the Hill

This may well be the king of tuned C4 Corvettes. It is certainly one of only four Lingenfelter twin-turbo ZR1 models. Under the hood rests a LT5 DOHC engine, tuned here to a stunning 850 hp. (Photograph © Jerry Heasley)

owner to order Lingenfelter twin-turbo ZR1s. However, Dehnert went one step further. He contracted with Lingenfelter to build no more than four of these twin turbos. A third twin turbo went to Houston, and the fourth is waiting to be built by custom order.

Lingenfelter made up special passenger-side dash plaques to denote each twin turbo is one of four built. Dehnert explained, "That little badge is one of the things Lingenfelter put together for us. He wanted it to be a special car, so he signed it and so did Graham Beham, an engineer who works for Lingenfelter and one of the original project engineers on the ZR1, working for Lotus. He's from England. So, he brought a tremendous amount of knowledge about the ZR1 and the development. He's been working for Lingenfelter for a couple years now."

Fitting the full-ball-bearing twin turbos into the engine bay was not an easy task. Probably the most difficult engineering work was packaging. Lingenfelter had to route the air to the turbos via stainless-steel pipes inside the frame. The turbos are hidden from the top. The engine bay looks pretty stock except for the big air box in the front, and you've got to put the car on a lift to view the turbos. Lingenfelter fabricated new exhaust manifolds that fit right up underneath the exhaust ports. The object was to get the turbos as close to the exhausts as possible to minimize turbo lag.

The DOHC LT5 retains the stock engineering features. Mainly, Lingenfelter upped the cubes to 368, cut back the compression ratio to 8.0:1, ported and polished the heads, changed to a turbo cam, installed special liners, and blueprinted the rotating masses.

The stock six-speed is equipped with a McCloud twin-disc clutch to handle the increased power. The suspension is also slightly modified for the awesome horses and torque. A special chip for the suspension controller flips the shocks to the soft setting, with no compression damping, so the rear end will squat for good weight transfer.

Dehnert commented, "If I don't have slicks on it you can be driving along in fourth gear at 50 mph and spin the rear tires, when the turbos spool up."

His best ET in the quarter mile is an eleven flat at 138 mph running Mickey Thompson ET streets, which Paul believes are almost as good as slicks.

Will Lingenfelter build more than four of these? This was a question posed at the ZR1 Gathering at Beech Bend Raceway during Lingenfelter's drag-

racing seminar. John said he was contractually committed to build only four unless Paul says differently. Until a hotter 'Vette comes along, C4 or C5, the Lingenfelter ZR1 twin turbo is apparently tuner king of the hill.

Rocket Roadster

"For my money, Chevy never built a classier looking 'Vette," Wayne Davis says of his '54 roadster.

But, like you and me and others who like to drive their old Corvettes, Davis wasn't much for the Powerglide two-speed behind the Stovebolt inline six. Adding a couple more cylinders wasn't a workable solution to cure the derivability of his '54, so Wayne attacked the root of the problem. He went after the chassis.

I met him at his shop as he returned from a short but quick drive. "How does she run, Wayne?"

"Oh man, like a brand-new one," Wayne answered. The suspension is C4, then fitted with wild 18x10 Centerlines in the back and 17x9s in the front. Power comes from a '68 Corvette 327 modified with dual quads.

Wayne, who is president of Regency Conversions in Ft. Worth, Texas, owns a restoration hobby shop in nearby Southlake where three employees build cars. Prior to going to work for Regency, Davis ran his own restoration shop in Odessa, Texas, for twenty-five years. His shop is full of rods, customs, muscle cars, and other iron. You're liable to see just about anything there.

With this '54 build, Wayne has really pushed his talents to the limit to create a rolling piece of artwork in fiberglass and steel. He had been dreaming of this car for years based on his affection for the first-generation Corvette. Davis is one of a breed of collectors who consider the 1953–1955 the most classic and raciest-looking Corvette of all time. The C1 was the marque's one and only true roadster, featuring side curtains in place of roll-up windows, and a lift-off softtop folding manually into a storage compartment behind the rear seats.

In these ways, the 1953–1955 'Vette copied the themes prevalent on postwar European sports cars, which were popular in the United States. The Blue Flame Six was standard power, and the foreign influence really shines through.

Wayne especially likes the stock wire headlight stone guards, the dual exhausts exiting bullet style through the rear valance, and the overall racy appear-

Rocket Roadster

A 1954 Corvette never looked so good. This retro 1954 custom began with a true 1954 Corvette, but retrofitted with modern Corvette parts. Power comes from a 1968 Corvette L79 327-ci (5,356-cc) V-8 producing 350 hp. The red leather is set off by 1959 Corvette Inca Silver paint. (Photograph © Jerry Heasley)

King Muscle 'Vette

Stock from top to bottom, this Rally Red 1966 Corvette convertible was powered by the 427-ci (6,994-cc) big-block. No customizing or modifications were even needed. (Photograph © Jerry Heasley)

ance of the body style. He especially likes the aggressiveness of the low, open mounted grille. Here, Wayne felt the car looked hotter without the license plate surround and bumper guards to either side.

Regency Conversions spent more than 300 hours block-sanding the body, which in Wayne's words was "awful, awful" when they started the work. When finished, Wayne believes Regency produced what is the best and straightest C1 Corvette on the planet.

Wayne thought long and hard about the color. He considered red and decided an original color option didn't fit this car's theme. Silver, being the look of polished steel and unavailable in 1954, emphasized the total mechanical renewal from the chassis up. Red leather set off the 1959 Corvette Inca Silver.

One more subtle modification to the exterior is difficult to spot. Notice the hood is not from a 1953–

1955, which is plain and flat. Wayne chose a 1957 hood that boasts a pair of raised bumps running lengthwise front to rear. They add a muscular look and integrate well with the corresponding bumps on top of the dash.

Wayne's upholsterer, Joe Romero, covered the stock seats and door panels with Connolly red leather and carpeted the floors with Mercedes Wilton Wool. If you can spot the one major difference inside, you know your early Corvettes: The steering wheel is a '57. The stock '54 wheel was Chevrolet passenger car with Corvette logo. On close inspection, you will also recognize the "Davis" logo on the gauge faces, a job Wayne farmed out to Carriage Works in Grand View, Missouri.

A four-speed manual was still three and a half years away from the Corvette option sheet in the dark ages of 1954. Wayne chose a shifter and shifter plate from a '68 Corvette.

Power comes from a '68 Corvette L79, the 350-horse 327, pumped up with a pair of Edelbrock 600s. The dual quads give Wayne's '54 a 1950s performance look. The distributor is stock '68 Corvette with dual points and a factory coil.

Aesthetics are important everywhere on this car, where a silver-and-red theme prevails. Notice the polished-aluminum Corvette valve covers set off by red. Kirk Cunningham at Carriage Works built the custom air cleaner, also silver and red. Allen-head screws secure the top from the bottom side so the fasteners are hidden for a clean look.

The master cylinder is a work of art. Cunningham cut back a GM dual reservoir to fit in the stock '54 location under the hood. In keeping with the simple hot rod V-8 build, there is no computer to engage the C4 ABS system, which is not present on this car. Carriage Works stamped the top of the master cylinder with the Davis logo.

Neither the C4 radiator fan nor the C4 steering system fit under the hood. Wayne hooked up an electric fan to the Bee Cool radiator and chose a Sweet Manufacturing rack-and-pinion steering system designed for sprint cars.

The most exotic changes are to the frame, modified at each end to accept the C4 underpinnings. The painted red 1954 frame's X-member is easy to recognize. Wayne powder-coated the aluminum C5 components Inca Silver to pop out against the red 1954 frame. The biggest job was cutting the halfshafts on the rear end to fit under the fenderwells, which are also modified to lie over the top of the A-frames. No off-the-shelf wheels fit inside the stock wells. Bob Devore at Centerline made four wheels from eight to get the offset right for a fit.

The result is a C4 '54 rocket roadster with a downright exotic character. The car is the best of three worlds: classic lines from the early 1950s, power from the muscle 1960s, and handling from the 1990s.

King Muscle 'Vette

Were you handed an option sheet today from 1966 and asked to check off boxes to build the highest-performance Corvette possible, you could do no better than this Rally Red convertible.

Roger Gibson has drag raced, street raced, and rebuilt now almost every series of hot muscle car, including Hemis, 427 'Vettes, LS-6 Chevelle, Six Pack Road Runners, you name it. After all that, he believes the 425-horse 427 Corvette is the strongest street muscle car ever built, even stouter than 435-horse Tri-Powers. "The 425-horse 427 is the ultimate street machine. That car will outrun Cobras. I think it is the fastest muscle car ever made for the street."

Those are strong words, but this is an awesome muscle car. In the November 1965 issue, *Car and Driver* tested a stock 425-horse 427 roadster, like the one seen here, and turned a 12.8 @ 112 mph in the quarter mile. They also posted a 0–60 mph time of 5.4 seconds, done with rather tame 3.36:1 rear-axle gears. These times are deceptively low considering first gear is apt to be mostly wheel spin with street tires, and it takes a patient throttle to attain maximum forward motion.

As far as outrunning the ultimate muscle car of all time, the Cobra, that same issue of *Car and Driver* tested a big-block 427 Cobra sports car, which was quicker through the quarter than the 'Vette. The main reason for this differential—427 Chevy versus 427 Ford—is that the Cobra weighed a half ton less! But, for the record, no other vintage, street muscle Corvette, with street tires, has ever turned a faster quarter mile ET in a magazine road test.

There are Corvette aficionados who rate the 425-horse 427 as King Muscle 'Vette. And they could be right.

★ ★ ★

And Then the Sun Came Out: Surviving the Open Road and Duntov's Own L-88

By Allan Girdler

It's amazing that we survive some of our escapades from our young and foolish years—especially when they include a ZL-1–tuned L-88 Corvette. Allan Girdler was an editor for *Car Life* in 1969 when he was entrusted with the keys to Zora Arkus-Duntov's own "skunkworks" Corvette and let loose on a journey he almost didn't get a chance to write about.

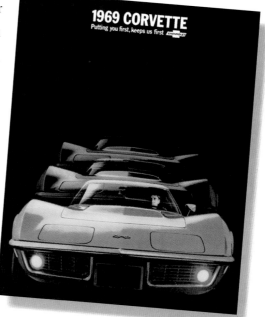

Facing page:
Breakfast of Champions
Classic 1960s T-shirt artwork in the best Rat Fink tradition.

Inset:
1969 Corvette Brochure

*n*ow, thirty-plus years later, I suspect I was too trusting in several ways, and that I fell victim to an urban legend. I probably should feel some regret . . . but I don't.

First, the legend. Back when General Motors had banned corporate involvement in racing and the top execs were being careful not to know the ban was being evaded, the top Corvette model was the L-88, a tuned 427-ci V-8 (what else?) with stiff suspension and no creature comforts. There was an option, with an aluminum engine block to go with the alloy heads and so forth, coded ZL-1, and the legend says guys who'd just made their fortunes would come into the Chevrolet agency and demand the most expensive Corvette the factory offered, the idea being the more you paid, the more you got, the more prestige came with the car.

Which was true in a way, with Cadillacs and Jaguars and the like, but with the Corvette, what the longest option list would bring was a racing car, a Corvette with 500 bhp to propel 3,000 pounds. The ZL-1 would win races, assuming the sanctioning bodies would cooperate, which they didn't, but the ZL-1 was nearly impossible to drive on the street. What I didn't know then, what was in fact a legend, was that the factory didn't build more than a handful of L-88s, and there's no way any rich dude off the street would have been told of the ZL-1, never mind sold one.

What I learned, and the point of this confession because I put that legend into print, was just what a wonderful, impossible beast the ZL-1 was.

In 1969, *Road & Track* magazine had a domestic companion publication, titled *Car Life*. The editor, Jim Hamilton, was an aggressive and inventive man, and he decided we (I was associate editor, second in command of a four-person office) would test every model Corvette in the 1969 line-up.

We found a loss leader, a baseline mild V-8 with three-speed stick, owned by a San Diego police officer. We asked Chevrolet for an L-88, and they did better, offering Zora Arkus-Duntov in person, along with his own mule, an L-88 tuned into a ZL-1, alloy block and heads, tuned exhaust, wide wheels and racing tires, every piece of racing equipment on the list, tuned and prepped by Duntov's guys in the skunkworks.

There was a mild problem, in that the car was in Los Angeles, and southern California was in the midst of the heaviest rainy season in recorded history. All the tracks were under water, so all the testing would have to be done in Arizona.

Duntov's car was set up for road racing, on wide, slick tires. All the radio and TV news could report was mudslides, floods, road closings.

The editor was a practical man. He had common sense, he said, but not all that much driving skill. The engineering editor was a licensed, winning pro driver, but didn't always think ahead.

But you, the editor said pointing to me, are a licensed driver who doesn't take chances, i.e. win races or crash, so you will drive the ZL-1 from LA to Phoenix.

Away I went, no heater, no defrost, no traction. Out of the city, into the mountains, hands light on the wheel, engine running at a fast, erratic idle, I managed to steer clear of any trouble.

Then we got to the mountain passes, still raining hard. I came over a crest and around a corner and there, maybe 100 yards ahead, were some cars. Sitting still. Waiting for the bulldozer to clear the mudslide.

There was no way I could stop in time.

All my life didn't flash before my eyes. Instead, I thought, Oh Geez, here I've got the job I've wanted since I was twelve, and I'm gonna lose it, wreck my career because I didn't have the sense to slow down, didn't have the brains God gives seafood.

Braking as hard as I could, I leaned forward, up against the steering wheel to minimize the impact.

The Corvette hit the mud and water. A giant wave sloshed over the windshield, blocking the view.

I came to a stop. I hadn't hit anything.

Silence.

I flipped on the wipers. The mud cleared off and I saw the cars driving away, on the other side of the slide. The flagman was standing, gaping, flag down. Had he seen me sliding down the hill and waved the crowd on?

I'll never know. I couldn't talk, couldn't look him in the eye, even. I put the car in gear and rumbled away, career intact despite my folly.

And then, speaking of folly, the sun came out.

We were in western Arizona, the wide open spaces, the open road below a blue sky, on a wide, straight road. I could see for miles . . . and there wasn't another car in sight.

This, I realized, was a chance I'd never had before, a 500-bhp Corvette geared for the open road, as fast a car as I'd ever get to drive, most likely, and here was the chance to see what the car would do, and let the car do what it was built to do.

So I put the pedal down.

Jack's

A 1965 Corvette convertible glistens under the neon lights of Jack's Liquor Store on Route 66 in Albuquerque, New Mexico.
(Photograph © Lucinda Lewis/All Rights Reserved)

Perhaps the best part is that there was no drama. The engine took on that hard, crisp note of a racing powerplant on song, the steering was precise, and the car tracked in harmony with me and the road.

I sat back and watched the needles, right to an indicated 165, and then I remembered, they have airplanes for people like me, so I eased off and cruised at merely illegal speeds, all the way to the track.

Duntov was his usual charming and informed self. He gave us the straight stuff while the PR man squirmed. He took me for a ride around the road course, rapped off a twelve-second quarter mile, and generally helped make the test the success it was.

Did I tell him how fast his car would go? I don't think so, mostly because it was a foolish thing to do.

Which isn't to say, given the chance, I wouldn't do it again.

"Road race"
A 1963 split-window Corvette coupe squares off against a 427 Shelby Cobra with a wide-open stretch of road waiting before them in this dreamy painting by artist Kent Bash. (Artwork © Kent Bash)

CHAPTER 5

Driving Off into the Sunset

1967 Corvette Convertible Hardtop

(Photograph © Jerry Heasley)

Vetteworld

By Floyd M. Orr

Floyd M. Orr is infatuated with automobiles and the power they exert on humanity. As a child growing up in Mississippi, he described himself as "a scrawny little kid who was always too thin to play any sport well." Instead, his mind wandered to dreams of cars.

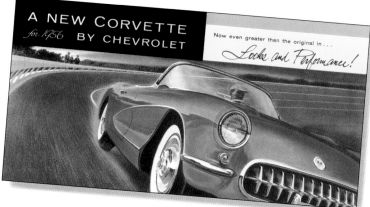

Floyd bought his first Corvette in 1980 when one day as he was driving down the road "a-mindin' my own business," he spotted an all-black 1969 L-36 Coupe for sale on the side of the road. The car "spoke to him," as Corvettes have a habit of doing, and he drove it home, sparking a lifelong love affair.

In 2000, Floyd compiled a series of his many essays on Corvettes and automobile culture into a book entitled *Plastic Ozone Daydream: The Corvette Chronicles*. He states that his writing style owes equal debts to Kurt Vonnegut, Anne Rice, and Peter Egan—an interesting blend of influences that all play a role in the following essay.

Facing page:
Split Window
The split rear window on the second-generation 1963 Corvette was a lightning rod of styling controversy upon its debut. (Photograph © Jerry Irwin)

Inset:
1956 Corvette Brochure

"But, Daaaaaad, I wanna go to Wally Wooorrrld. . . !"

"Quit whining, Rusty. We went there last year and it was a disaster! All we saw was a fat security guard and a stupid *"Closed for Repairs"* sign!"

"Only 'cause you didn't call first . . ."

"Don't you smart off to me, son. We're going to Vetteworld this year. It's all over the TV that they just opened at the end of April and they're packing 'em in! It's the only theme park in the world just for us car lovers and it's just down the road near San Marcos. You'll love it, kid!"

"Are we going in the Corvette, Dad?"

"Of course not, son. That's over two-hundred miles from here, and where would your mother and sister ride, in the hatch? We'll take the Lumina APV."

"That's the stupidest name for a car I ever heard. We'll have to park that stupid thing a hunnerd miles from the front gate! They let all the Corvettes park up close. That's what they say on TV!"

Vetteworld does indeed have a split parking lot. All Corvettes park in what has been billed as the largest covered lot in Texas, located directly approaching the front gate, and all other vehicles are directed into the normally designed, humongous lot located some distance from the gate. This horde of visitors will ride a tram decorated with huge facsimiles of big black-and-white cows, through the lot of plastic beasties, up to the main gate. The Corvettes are protected by barriers and guards, of course, and the hordes are not complaining because the tram ride is quite scenic. On a nice day the scenery rivals the average National Corvette Convention. All Corvette drivers to the park get a five-dollar discount off the ticket prices. Cows? What cows? Oh yes, Vetteworld has Blue Bell as a sponsor (more on this later).

Let's satisfy the little kids and old codgers first by touring Pioneer Land. Every theme park has its little putt-putt type cars to drive, and this area has more than any other park. All the cars are seriously styled and designed to replicate Corvettes of the vintage years, 1953–62, in a 2/3-scale format. It may seem simple at first, but the development and engineering involved rivaled the famous robot clones of Disney World! Kids of all ages above five can experience Corvettes of all the solid-axle variations. The controls, suspension, tires and even the colors are all authentic. While Grandpa is

racing his delighted grandchildren from apex to apex at speeds which seem much greater than they are, Mom and Dad visit the museum chock full of artifacts from the '53–'62 era, and later they sit on a park bench and watch the kids. Bench sitting in the park is best appreciated while eating the best apple pie a la mode in the world. Made by Blue Bell and overpriced beyond

Stingray

In 1959, Harley Earl's heir apparent, Bill Mitchell, built his futuristic Stingray test mule on the final Corvette SS chassis and clothed it in a body designed by Peter Brock. The Stingray would become influential on the second generation of Corvettes—although they would bear the name Sting Ray. (Photograph © Jerry Heasley)

belief, this delight is served upside-down in a big cup for munching on the hoof or rightsideup for patio consumption. Like a 1992 Corvette, it is expensive and tasty, and all the other apple pies and sports cars are indeed looking upward. Before departing Pioneer Land we must splash down the ubiquitous log-jam of sliding modules shaped like the boats of Corvette namesake.

The next stop on our day-long march is Fantasy Land, featuring the fantasy objects of most visitors, the '63–'67 Sting Rays, and sponsored by Castrol. The main attraction in Fantasy Land is the world's only sooper-dooper-fast oil slide! The mile-long line waiting for this treat moos its way through a corral featuring classic car tunes to speed the passing of the waiting time. A tape that lasts about as long as the wait includes "Route 66," "Dead Man's Curve," "Little Red Corvette," "I Get Around," and "The Little Old Lady from Pasadena." Thrill seekers ride a molded plastic bobsled sort of vehicle down a steep drop into a series of switchbacks leading to a sudden climb and a very specially designed hydraulic braking system. The sled rides on a thin film of carefully blended Castrol and it reaches speeds approaching those of the supercoasters. All riders are given a computer printed time slip denoting their personal trip at the end of each slide. The best place to unwind after this oily 75-second experience is The Chevy Show. Vetteworld purchased the contract on this aural delight from Six Flags, contracted Bose to design the sound system, and changed the format to display only simulated rides in various types of Corvettes. Aside from these and a few minor rides, Fantasy Land features a small amphitheater for visiting guest speakers of the obvious variety and a Sixties Museum containing the rarest examples of Sting Rays that money could buy at any price. Each car is enclosed within glass and has a video displaying that particular car's detailed history and specifications.

Most theme parks have some sort of *tunnel of monsters* ride suitable for kids of most ages. This one starts right under the gigantic crossed flags of Adventure Land, sponsored by Exxon and featuring all fifteen model years of the Stingrays. The ride consists of fifteen separate pseudo-cars towed along with hydraulics and electricity, through a maze of dark tunnels. This unoriginal concept display frightens the brave patrons with critters of a different sort. Door bangers pop out of their cars impersonating ordinary citizens. The car rolls over a surface made of bricks and potholes. Seagulls and pigeons are perched overhead all along the route. A constant symphony of chirps and squawks from radar detectors assaults the ears. Images of Cobras suddenly leap from the dark walls. The wheezing racket of air-cooled, six-cylinder OHC engines drone through the elaborate sound system when least expected. Following this trail of terror, most park visitors head straight for the Stingray café where the specialty is *Mako Shark on a Stick*.

Two things usually compose the bottom line of what draws the zillions of park visitors year after year, and one of these is located in Adventure Land. The *L-88* is a supercoaster from the old school. Constructed entirely of wood and painted all American red and white, the cars of this coaster are shaped in the image, when viewed as a whole, of one very long red 1969 L-88 with black interior. The track itself is white and the upholstery of the cars is black vinyl. The ride is bumpy but extremely fast and exciting. The roar emanating from the wheels is unprecedentedly loud and the acceleration down the first hill is not the quickest in the world, but the noise and harshness of the ride certainly make it seem to be the fastest. Patrons exiting this wild beast underneath the red, white, and blue Exxon sign are usually rattled and satiated.

The next stop is usually the Tomorrow Land Museum, which features some of the rarest and most precious of the non-production Corvettes of the past. Included are the original racing Sting Ray, the Mako Shark show car, the Duntov SS, the XP-887, and the Two and Four Rotor Wankel Corvette experimental cars. The Tomorrow Land sponsor is Goodyear and the Corvettes featured are all the post-Stingray models. After a ride on the *L-88*, most people don't mind a quiet wait in the corral for the row of specially programmed computers with printers lined up for eager fingers. Loaded with all the option codes for all the years and models of Corvettes, these PC's will spit out the individual's choice of a Corvette of any kind displayed in a dealer window-sticker format suitable for framing. After this pedestrian experience, it is time to walk the black circular corral, the largest in the park, which leads to a trip on the blackest, meanest, highest, fastest, longest, quickest, cold-steel supercoaster in the universe, the *ZR-1*. Although most all the supercoasters now in theme parks nationwide were engineered by rollercoaster design firms, the *ZR-1* has been engineered jointly by a coaster specialist firm and the entire Corvette ZR-1 / LT -5 development team. This is indeed the central calling card of Vetteworld. . . .

The *ZR-1* is best experienced after dark, when the exclusive light show of bright white halogens and aircraft landing lights which emanates from within the structure of the coaster track effectively distorts the whole experience into a fantasy never to be forgotten. Passengers squeeze their buns into tight-fitting black vinyl sportseats with racing-type three-point shoulder belts strapping them into place. The parallel hand grips are vertical bars of thick black vinyl which simulate the grip of a steering wheel and the riders can brace their legs with rubber foot pads positioned like brake and throttle pedals. The *ZR-1* drops off that first hill like a Ford dropped from a cargo plane, only to rush up the first climb like a rocket blasting off. The next downhill leads into a curve only a Lotus Elan could love, then it switches back to the other direction as if the driver was paid by an ambulance chaser specializing in whiplash. The next uphill is a little slower than the first, but this perception is deceiving because the crest of the hill leads into a barrel roll through a pitch-black cave! This little downhill surprise is followed by three Lotus-inspired S-curves and an upside-down path up the next hill, which becomes an over-the-hood-ornament backward loop! The final downhill appears to glide to a smooth halt, but the truth is that it is smooth all right, but the final deceleration is actually as quick as multi-wheel disc brakes will allow, featuring the latest in *antiupchuck* technology!

"Well, Rusty, wouldn't that be better than any old Wally World? We would have driven all the way to the West Coast just to see a silly moose probably made in Japan, instead of staying right here in Texas and seeing stuff made completely in Ammurrica!"

"Yeah, Dad. Even stoopid old girls like those putt-putt rides. Next year let's take the Vette and make them ride in the hatch! With the ten-buck discount we can buy two extra helpings of apple pie. . . ."

The street was deserted late Friday night
We were buggin' each other while we sat out the light
We both popped the clutch when the light turned green
You shoulda heard the whine from my screamin' machine
Dead Man's Curve, I can hear 'em say:
"Won't come back from Dead Man's Curve"
—Jan and Dean's "Dead Man's Curve," 1964

Save the Wave!

Waving to fellow Corvette drivers has long been a rite. This tradition acknowledges other Corvette owners in a sort of secret handshake of the road. This quaint essay from the August/September 1969 *Corvette News* offers advice on the many different types of waves that you may choose to give to your fellow "Vetterans."

Ever since Corvette No. 00001 first met Corvette No. 00002 on the road, their drivers saluted each other with waves. Today, unfortunately, this grand and glorious tradition is wavering.

There's one item of standard equipment that comes as a pleasant surprise to every new Corvette owner. It's the instant wave of recognition he receives when he meets one of his ilk on the road. The first time it happens, he is taken by surprise. He immediately thinks: (1) he has been mistaken for Sterling Moss; (2) His lights are on; or (3) He has just been given the bird.

Soon, however, the new Vette owner anticipates, indeed even relishes, encountering other Vettes as he drives. During this period, he experiments with his waves, running the gamut from the gaping "yoo hoo" to the ultra-cool "two-finger flip." He perfects his timing, making sure he affects neither the too-eager, too-early wave, nor the jaded "oh brother" too-late variety. Determined not to be one upped, he even develops a defense mechanism for non-wavers, usually settling on the "Wave? My hand was just on the way to scratch my head" approach. (This is especially useful when you're not driving your Vette, but you forget, and like a dummy, wave anyway.)

Indeed, one of the most perplexing problems facing a would-be waver is what to do when driving next to a fellow Vette owner. Passing him going in opposite directions is one thing. Greetings are exchanged, and that's that. But what happens when you pull up next to a guy at a light, wave, nod, smile and then pull up next to him at the next light, a block later? Wave again? Nod bashfully? Grin self-consciously? Ignore him? Or take the chicken's way out and turn down the next side street? If you're expecting an answer, you won't find it here. Sad to say, some questions don't have any.

Girl-type Corvette drivers also have a unique problem: to wave or not to wave. The miss or misses who borrows her man's Corvette for the first time is immediately faced with this quandary. Should she wave first and look overly friendly, or ignore the wave and look like a snob? Most ladies who drive their own Vettes prefer to suffer the latter rather than take the chance of being misread. For this reason, all girls are excused for occasionally failing to return a well-meaning wave. So are new owners who are still learning the ropes.

There is no excuse, however, for the guy who refuses to return a wave, not out of ignorance, but of arrogance or apathy. While this type of behavior is the exception to the rule, it seems that a few owners of newer models refuse to recognize anything older than theirs, while some others simply won't wave, period. Boo on them. These ding-a-lings don't seem to realize that they are helping to quash a tradition that had its beginnings back when most of us were still driving Tootsietoys. And besides, in this era of mechanized anonymity, we need to save all the human relationships we can.

What to do about the problem of non-wavers? Well, in the movie *The Hustler,* Fast Eddie had his hands broken for not playing by the rules. But, maybe this is going just a bit too far. Maybe the solution is to cure these guys with kindness.

So . . . pick a wave you like. Then, the next time you pass a fellow Vetteran, make sure you use it. And the next time. And the next. Who knows? If you don't succeed in getting some of these hard-noses to wave back, at least you'll have the satisfaction of knowing that you've started a lot of them thinking. And that alone is worth a wave.

1958 Corvette Dealer Promotional Postcard

The Gaping "Yoo Hoo!": Good for waving at Vettes on the other side of divided highways, in medium-to-heavy traffic. Not much good for anything else.

The Two-Finger Flip: A move that can say "Hi." Or "Wow!" Or "Victory." Or most anything else, depending on the action of the giver, and the reaction of the taker.

The Four-Finger Pop-up: One of the classics. Palm grasps top of wheel, while fingers are extended snappily. An inscrutable expression helps the total effect.

The Eight-Point Spread: Broad, expansive and outgoing. The hand action is reminiscent of Al Jolson at his best.

The Pointer: Sort of a wink, a click and a "bang, you're dead!" combination. Can also be used to draw attention to a pursuing traffic cop, in which case, you are dead.

The Wiping Swipe: Sort of a "Hi, guys." Primarily given by patronizing father-figure types.

The Topper-Tipper: A rarely seen, but eloquent gesture. Can prove embarrassing when the tipper wears both a hat and a toupee.

The Right-Handed "Hi-G'Bye": A desperation move, given only at the last minute. Hand shoots straight skyward, occasionally scrunching fingernails or knuckles in the process.

The Near-Futile Head Jerk: A last resort, when you think you'll be snubbed, but aren't; or when you think you haven't been daydreaming, but have.

The Last-Minute Left Elbow Grope: Another desperation tactic, usually seen only in rear-view mirrors. Has all the grace and finesse of a peg-legged man in a forest fire.

The Saga of 003

By Mike Antonick with John C. Amgwert

John Amgwert's grandfather bought the first 1930 Model A Ford sold in the city of Lincoln, Nebraska. Forty years later, John and his dad thought it would be neat to buy back that Model A and restore it. Despite its decrepit condition, the Ford's owners wouldn't part with it. To soothe the disappointment, John searched frantically for a suitable substitute, something old and unusual. Word of mouth led to a 1954 Corvette, and $1,900 cash bought it.

In the early 1970s, nobody—including Chevy dealers—knew much about these early Corvettes, so owners started getting together to share information. This led to the formation of the National Corvette Restorers Society in 1974 by seven men. John was one. The organization grew and prospered, and the membership now exceeds 15,000.

At the time NCRS was founded, John worked for the Roller Skating Rink Operator's Association of America in a little in-house print shop. With this link to the printing trade, John was the logical choice to produce a club newsletter. John ended up being the editor-in-chief for *The Corvette Restorer* magazine's first twenty-five years.

John's appetite for research led to a minority ownership stake in the earliest Corvette known to exist, the third production 1953 Corvette built. Here is the saga of that car's purchase in 1987 with John's documentary research that cracked the mysteries of its clouded past.

1953 Corvette 003

Corvette serial number 003 today following restoration by Southwestern Restorations shop in Tulsa, Oklahoma. (Photograph © John C. Amgwert)

A little knowledge can be dangerous, but a lot can be downright disastrous. Consider the situation three Corvette enthusiasts faced as they examined what was purported to be the earliest Corvette in existence: 1953 serial number E53F001003, the third Corvette ever produced.

The site was the Rick Cole Auction Company's classic car auction held at Monterey, California, on August 21, 1987. The three men—Les Bieri of Virginia, Howard Kirsch of Oklahoma, and John Amgwert of Nebraska—weren't Corvette novices. All three already owned 1953 models. Between them, Bieri and Kirsch had another forty-one Corvettes in their personal collections. Amgwert's 1953 was one of four Corvettes he owned at the time, and this guy was a walking, talking Corvette encyclopedia. Since 1971, he's been editor of *The Corvette Restorer* magazine, the highly technical, award-winning quarterly member publication of the National Corvette Restorer's Society. Among the elite group of those who really understood the nuances of early Corvette production, these men were heavyweights.

They hadn't come to Monterey for the auction. Popular vintage auto races are held each August at Laguna Seca raceway near Monterey, and the 1987 races featured Chevrolet as the honored marque because 1987 was Chevrolet's seventy-fifth anniversary. Chevrolet dusted off old one-of-a-kind Corvettes, and privately owned Corvettes of every age and description were also expected. It all added up to a once-in-a-lifetime treat no Corvette nut could miss, so the NCRS scheduled its annual meet in Monterey to coincide with the festivities. It was the NCRS meet that brought Bieri, Kirsch, and Amgwert to town.

Rick Cole auctions are glittering events with rare Ferraris, Cobras, and other exotics pulling in the big-money investor crowd. Corvettes are joining this elite company, but E53F001003 looked sadly out of place waiting its turn to cross the auction block. It couldn't be driven, and its rough-looking, unrestored condition surely prompted more than one of the immaculately dressed high rollers to wonder what in heaven's name it was doing there.

Les Bieri knew. He knew that in 1969, *Corvette News,* Chevrolet's in-house predecessor to *Corvette Quarterly,* had, at the suggestion of a reader, conducted a search to locate all remaining 1953 Corvettes. Each owner was asked to send tracings of the vehicle identification number plate, the metal tag screwed into the driver-side door hinge pillar of each 1953 model. For their trouble, bona fide 1953 owners would receive sterling silver engraved fascia plates, and the owner of the earliest Corvette to surface would receive a fourteen-carat gold plate. The December-January 1970 *Corvette News* published the results: The "winner" was Ed Thiebaud of Fresno, California, with the 1953 serial number E53F001003.

Now here was the same Ed Thiebaud at Monterey, standing beside the same Number Three Corvette, ready to sell it to the highest bidder.

Bieri was determined to have it. In his opinion, this was potentially the most valuable Corvette in existence. It won't be too long before a 1961 Corvette Grand Sport changes hands for $1 million, but there are five of those. There's only *one* earliest Corvette. Yet, Kirsch and Amgwert tried to talk their friend out of what they initially felt would be a terrible mistake,

Why? Because this old Number Three was one controversial puzzle of a Corvette. Here's where the extraordinary expertise of these men—too much knowledge, maybe—worked against them: It nearly prevented them from deciding to join forces and go after Number Three.

To understand their misgivings, one must know the nature of the Corvette's birth and early days. From 1949 through 1961, General Motors previewed its new model to major markets around the country with its extravagant Motoramas. To spice things up, a few "dream cars" were often included. It was as a Motorama dream car that the Corvette first appeared in January 1953, at the Waldorf-Astoria in Manhattan. The official Chevrolet statement after that showing was that the Corvette had caused such a commotion, there was no choice but to rush it into production to meet demand. Well, the commotion caused by the Corvette was real enough, but it's now known that Chevrolet Chief Engineer Ed Cole planned all along to add Corvettes to Chevrolet showrooms. One giveaway is that the Motorama Corvette wasn't the typical dream car "pushmobile," it was a fully operational, pre-production pilot car.

Perhaps to avoid losing the momentum generated by the Motorama showings, Cole ordered a few hundred (it turned out to be exactly 300) Corvettes built before the end of 1953 for sale to the public as 1953 models. This was one aggressive schedule, as the Cor-

American Style

The 1961 Corvette received a subtle design facelift and became seen around the world as the epitome of classic American sports car style. (Photograph © Jerry Heasley)

vette was no more than an idea in 1951 and just a plaster model as late as May 1952. What made it possible was the Corvette's revolutionary fiberglass body, because the dies necessary for stamping steel panels would have taken much longer to design and build than the relatively simple dies required to produce plastic panels.

These first Corvettes were built slowly, mostly by hand, in a converted Van Slyke Avenue warehouse in Flint, Michigan. Meanwhile, an assembly plant was being readied in St. Louis to produce, starting in 1954, at least 10,000 Corvettes per year.

This figure turned out to be wildly optimistic, but that's another story. What's important here is the handbuilt nature of 1953 Corvettes and the running changes that occurred with practically every one built. Chevrolet was doing the impossible: It was building production Corvettes at the same time it was developing the tooling with which to build them! Naturally, quality generally improved with each 1953 made. But, as owners of these relics learned through years of com-

paring their cars, hundreds of components and assembly practices changed as those first 300 Corvettes were gingerly put together.

This was the crux of the problem with E53F001003. Bieri, Kirsch and Amgwert could see that some of the components just weren't representative of early 1953 production. For example, the softtop mechanism was a 1953 all right, but it was the *later* of the two styles. The plastic side window curtains were date-coded too late.

The brake lines of 1953 Corvettes were attached to the outboard edge of the right-hand frame rails before being relocated to the inboard edge early in 1954 production. Number Three's brake lines were mounted inboard. The engine block number wasn't correct for a 1953 model.

Disturbing enough, but there was more. The VIN of every production Corvette, right from the start, has been stamped into its frame during assembly. In 1978, a frame stamped E53F001003, the frame that *should* have been under Thiebaud's Corvette body, was dis-

"Corvette Doctor"

A lonely garage promises Corvette "doctoring" in this painting by Dale Klee. (Artwork © Dale Klee)

covered in Michigan mated to a 1955 Corvette as it was being restored by its owner, Phil Havens. Amgwert knew all too well about the frame. Sam Folz, the late NCRS president and technical director, had photographed and described it to Amgwert, and he told the story in the Fall 1978 issue of *The Corvette Restorer*. Thiebaud nixed requests to have his Corvette inspected, so rumors started flying. Was Thiebaud's car a fraud? Was it a nothing-special Corvette with Number Three's VIN plate attached? Was the VIN plate itself a counterfeit?

At Monterey that fateful day, Kirsch and Amgwert did their best to persuade Bieri to pass on this one. It was too tainted, too risky. Bieri knew his friends' concerns were solid, but he couldn't walk away from Number Three just yet. Hours remained before the Corvette would be auctioned, so the three men started talking with Thiebaud.

Thiebaud recalled that he'd bought the Corvette in 1969 from a man in Hollydale, California. He said the Corvette had been stored for several years before he bought it because it wouldn't run. He'd trailered it to his farm and never changed a piece of the car the

before and a few that were typical of later production. The frame still had them stumped. Even though the brake lines weren't located properly for a 1953, it sure looked tight otherwise, and there was no evidence it had been tampered with since leaving Flint. The more they looked, the more excited the Corvette trio became.

Finally Amgwert, goosebumps rising on his arms, said, "Fellas, I can't explain some of these things, but it's the oldest Corvette I've ever seen. I think it's real!"

Since it was Bieri who wanted to buy Number Three from the beginning, he was to do the bidding. He'd rounded up $32,000 and set that as the limit he could pay. Kirsch said, I don't think that'll buy it. If you can get it for that, it's yours. But if it takes more, I'll put up the difference plus the cost of the restoration." Kirsch had to leave before the Corvette was auctioned to pick up his daughter at the airport.

When he returned, Bieri greeted him with a big grin and a "Hi, partner." It took $37,000 plus commission. Amgwert then asked if he could be a minority partner, in his words, "even if I just owned a taillight," to be a part of what he was now convinced would be one of the great all-time Corvette stories. Bieri and Kirsch immediately agreed, realizing that if anyone could crack the mysteries of E53F001003, it would be Amgwert and his contacts within the Corvette hobby.

The pieces of the puzzle started fitting together slowly. In 1978, when Amgwert researched the article about the E53F001003 frame in Michigan, he had found a photo in *Motor Trend* of Mr. and Mrs. Thiebaud with Number Three, showing the front California license plate, FIH657. Plates stay with cars in California after changes of ownership, so the California Department of Motor Vehicles was able to find a previous owner, Sharon L. Crockett.

After Monterey, Amgwert passed this information on to Kirsch, who stopped at the last known address of Sharon Crockett to see if anyone there might know what happened to her. John L. Crockett, Sharon's ex-husband, still resided at the address. He'd sold the Corvette to Thiebaud, and he remembered it oh so well.

Crockett bought the Corvette from a used car dealer in Lynwood, California, in 1958, for $1,200. He thought it had been wholesaled to the used car dealer by yet another dealer.

Crockett drove the 1953 Corvette less than 5,000 miles from 1958 to 1963. During a trip in 1963, the Powerglide transmission wouldn't upshift to high gear,

entire time he'd owned it. He'd never even driven it. Asked about the frame, Ed Thiebaud said it had *no* numbers where Corvette frames normally did and he had no explanation.

Contrary to their preconceived notions, Bieri, Kirsh and Amgwert found Thiebaud seemingly open and honest, even permitting the trio to crawl around and under the car, and to disassemble and inspect the headlight buckets, grill and taillights. As they probed, it became clear it was unquestionably a very early 1953. The engine block casting number was wrong, but all else in the engine bay, including the cylinder head, checked out. There were some weird pieces they hadn't seen and Crockett limped home in low gear, parked the car, covered it with a tarp, and never drove it again. It remained unlicensed from 1963 until he sold it to Thiebaud around 1969. Crockett remembered Thiebaud calling very late one night, asking if it was for sale and what the serial number was. Crockett had his daughter go out to the car several times with a flashlight to read and confirm the serial number while he spoke to Thiebaud on the phone.

Crockett remembered positively the VIN number as E53F001003, and that he had thought it meant it was the 1,003rd Corvette made in 1953. It wasn't until after he'd sold the car that he realized it was the *third* Corvette made. He also recalled the Corvette having a "California Replacement" engine block. (The block is stamped N364400CAL, with a casting date of C128-March 12, 1958.) Crockett said this was the engine in the car when he bought it in 1958, and he didn't change it. According to Thiebaud, Crockett never liked V-8s.

Both Crockett and Thiebaud said the Corvette had not been driven since 1963. Today the odometer shows 72,356.2 miles. That would put the mileage at about 67,000 when Crockett bought it in 1958 as a five-year-old used car. Since December 31, 1963, the car has been considered a "non-operating" motor vehicle by the state of California, further verification of both Crockett's and Thiebaud's recollections. Thiebaud has stated emphatically that he did nothing to the Corvette in all the years he owned it.

Well, almost nothing. There was that time he buried it underground. He did this by bulldozing a hole into the side of a mountain and supporting the opening with huge timbers. He then covered the car with plastic and vented the opening before covering the hole back up again. According to Thiebaud's comments to Kirsch, the idea was sort of to make it disappear for a while during divorce proceedings. But apparently the sale of the car at the Rick Cole auction in Monterey finally settled the divorce.

In addition to all this information, a California title expert retained by the Rick Cole Auction Company deciphered the title's "00/00/53" as meaning this car was first sold in California during the 1953 calendar year, and a code "AY" as indicating that the sale price was more than $3,500.

So our Three Musketeers knew their Corvette was sold as new or near new sometime in 1953 in California, and that it had racked up roughly 67,000 miles by

1958 when Crockett bought it. Five years and 5,000 miles later, Number Three got an early retirement.

Kirsch trailered the Corvette back to his shop in Oklahoma, and soon Bieri and Amgwert joined him for a very careful disassembly and investigation. What they found was documented with photography and extensive notes, and other Corvette owners and early-Corvette experts were invited to look and comment. The idea was to both share this car with other enthusiasts and seek help in cracking the many mysteries still remaining.

What they found astonished everyone. While it needed complete restoration, Number Three was an excellent original; it was remarkably complete. The exhaust system had never been changed. Dated components such as the starter, distributor, water pump, windshield, rear spring assemblies, axle, radiator, heater core, transmission adapter, and cylinder head were all compatible with July 1953 production. Many components—like the ignition shielding, bullet air cleaners, cowl vent, grille bar, gas filler door, and stainless trim—were hand-fabricated, as expected with a very early 1953. Trim pieces like the grille teeth and side "gull wings" were rough castings, some in bronze instead of the pot metal used in later 1953 models. The bronze grille teeth in Number Three, for instance, weighed eight pounds more than the pot metal teeth of Howard Kirsch's 1953, serial number E53F001225. After a complete teardown, the only components found not to be 1953 Corvette were the voltage regulator, a larger inside rearview mirror, replacement Gabriel shock absorbers, the engine short block, and the tires.

The fiberglass body was all hand-laid cloth, certainly one of the first. It had a one-piece underbody, common only to the first eighteen or twenty Flint Corvettes. Stripping the paint revealed that the only body repair was in the rear, below the trunk lid. It was an amateur job, done with the body on the frame; hardened plastic resin was still adhered to the rear frame cross member.

The VIN plate was removed and compared with those of two other early Corvettes, E53F001005 and E53F001006. The three were identical, right down to the tooling imperfections.

What about the frame? Just as Thiebaud had said, there were no stamped numbers to correspond to the VIN tag. No question it was an early 1953 frame, though. Careful removal of the dirt and grease revealed

First Three Corvettes

Tony Kleiber, a body assembler, prepares to drive Corvette serial number 001 off the small Flint, Michigan, pilot assembly line on Friday morning, June 30, 1953. Standing alongside the car is R. G. Ford, general manager of Chevrolet Assembly Plants, and F. J. Fessenden, Flint plant manager. The body of Corvette 003 was being installed on the chassis in the background. (Chevrolet photo courtesy of John C. Amgwert)

Mirror Image

A 1956 Corvette convertible reflects in the still waters below it. The year marked the first body redesign for the Corvette, creating a sleeker, more streamlined look than the premiere, 1953–1955 Corvettes. This car featured the optional AM radio, which was transistorized—another Corvette first. (Photograph © Jerry Heasley)

the date code, 6.18.53, stenciled on by the frame's manufacturer, A. O. Smith Corporation. It had handmade gussets reinforcing the forward support of the rear springs on both sides. All 1953 Corvettes had reinforcing gussets, but not quite like these.

The rear axle was coded LW519, which corresponds to a 1953 Corvette 3.55:1 ratio, assembled May 19. The rear spring assemblies were both dated E3 (May 1953). Both the rear axle and spring codes exactly match those of the fifth Corvette built, E53F001005.

Remember the business about the brake lines running along the inside of the frame rail, instead of outside, like other 1953 and early 1954 models? Close inspection proved that the lines had originally been on the outside of the frame rail but had been *moved* inboard. It was done by hand (the frame holes showed evidence of hand drilling, not machine punching), but very professionally, and couldn't have been done with the body on the frame.

Two other bits of evidence suggested this frame was factory installed and hadn't been touched since. First, the axle rebound straps were in place with factory-type rivets and hadn't been disturbed. It's extremely difficult to remove an early Corvette's rear axle from its frame without cutting these loose. Second, it was normal Corvette factory practice to hold the body mount rubber cushions and metal shims in position with 114-inch-wide tape before the body was dropped on. The tape was still there. Heavens, was it really the oldest Corvette?

Based on their own findings and the opinions of others who viewed the car, the Bieri-Kirsch-Amgwert team speculated that the frame with their Corvette must have been a "mule" (experimental) frame used for testing and fitting the modified spring gussets, the relocated brake fines, and other engineering "improvements." And, they reckoned, this frame was installed by Chevrolet prior to the Corvette's being shipped to a retail customer. If the frame Phil Havens found under his 1955 Corvette was numbered correctly and was originally under Number Three, then Chevrolet must have removed it and replaced it with the modified frame.

Speculation is one thing. Proof is quite another. Without some kind of hard documentation, Corvette Number Three would never be more than an interesting collection of old Corvette parts combined with the earliest-known Corvette VIN plate. The more Bieri, Kirsch and Amgwert researched their car, the more confident they were it was the real McCoy. They really had the earliest Corvette in existence—they just couldn't prove it . . . yet.

Earlier in 1988, a GM employee called Amgwert after reading an article about the controversy swirling around Number Three. The anonymous contact asked Amgwert to send everything he could about the car, and he'd check to see if any records still existed.

On June 6, 1988, the contact called Amgwert and said, "You'd better sit down!"

Extensive documents tracing E53F001003 had been located. After being built at Flint, it became General Motors Car Development Engineering Staff car ES-127. In other words, it *was* retained as an engineering mule, just as the expert threesome had guessed. An inch-thick stack of documents spelled out the details. Would Bieri, Kirsch and Amgwert care to journey to Detroit to inspect the documents?

You bet.

They arrived at Chevrolet-Pontiac-Canada (CPC) headquarters on June 16, 1988. It's a day they'll never forget.

When it was a week old, Number Three was driven from GM's Main Engineering Center in Warren, Michigan, to Harrison Radiator in Lockport, New York, for fourteen hours of cold shake tests at -20 degrees Fahrenheit. A two-page report detailed the procedures that were followed and the conclusions they reached.

Furthermore, on August 20, 1953, Chevrolet Engineering issued a work order for the purpose of "Reconditioning Technical Center Corvette which has completed 5,000 miles on Belgian Block." This was the needle-in-the-haystack document that explained it all. The exact phrasing of the work order was as follows:

"Technical Center test car ES-127 (#3 production Corvette) has completed 5,000 miles on the Belgian

Blocks. This work order is being issued to recondition the car and to make the various fixes that have been found necessary on regular production cars.

"This will also cover the chassis work required. Technical Center will replace the frame and steering mechanism; therefore, no work is to be done on those items."

The following day a supplemental work order was issued. It directed Chevrolet Engineering to obtain and furnish to the General Motors Technical Center a new frame and other parts. All of Number Three's other deviations from typical early 1953 production were thus explained in the documentation Chevrolet provided.

Number Three is being restored to the state in which it left Warren following reconditioning. But there's still more to learn. The latest document obtained from Chevrolet was dated October 26, 1953. The car's history from then until John Crockett's purchase in 1958 is unknown.

There's still Phil Havens's E53F001003 frame. Did Chevrolet keep it and install it later under another Corvette? Or was it scrapped, only to mysteriously surface twenty-five years later?

And what of the first two built, E53F001001 and E53F001002? Were they scrapped in tests, as has been rumored for years? Since there were two Motorama Corvettes, did Chevrolet actually start the VIN numbers at Flint with E53F001003? Or are they still hiding somewhere, waiting for the luckiest car enthusiast alive to find them?

One thing is for sure: If they are found it'll be by someone like Les Bieri, who listened to his heart instead of cold, hard facts, to make the Corvette deal of the decade.

What has become of 003 since?

The car was meticulously disassembled and restored by Lloyd Miller at Howard Kirsch's Southwestern Restorations shop in Tulsa, Oklahoma. The completed chassis was first displayed at the NCRS regional meet at Bend, Oregon, in 1989. The first showing of the completed vehicle was at the NCRS regional meet at Scottsdale, Arizona, in May 1990. Acquiring the NCRS's prestigious Duntov Award requires a 97 percent static judging score plus Performance Verification which is a road test to check function of all mechanical

components. This Corvette scored a 99 percent at Scottsdale and passed the Performance Verification with flying colors. The Duntov Award was presented at the NCRS's 1990 national meet at Williamsburg, Virginia.

Perhaps 003's ultimate honor was its display at GM's Technical Center in Warren, Michigan, in June 1990. 003 also spent time in the Chevrolet Central Office lobby at CPC (Chevrolet-Pontiac-Canada) headquarters, and at GM Design Staff. The car was driven on the Tech Center's test track. This may have been the only time a privately owned vehicle was displayed and driven at this facility. The employees of the Tech Center could be excused for being a little jaded—they're exposed to all manner of exciting vehicles—but 003 created a absolute sensation. Howard Kirsch, Les Bieri, and John Amgwert were with the car at all times, and each remembered having the time of his life.

Partnerships have a way of souring, but these men always got along splendidly. Sadly, though, Howard Kirsch died in 1994. That took the fun out of it all for Les Bieri, and he sold his 003 interest to the Kirsch family trust in 1998. Amgwert remains a minority owner.

003 does continue to entertain the public from time to time. It has made appearances at the Bloomington Gold Special Collection; at the Palace in Auburn Hills, Michigan, for a GM engineering symposium; at the Texas State Fair for a month; and it spent 2002 at the National Corvette Museum in Bowling Green, Kentucky.

This is a car that Corvette enthusiasts have talked about since it surfaced in that 1970 *Corvette News* search. It continues to lay claim to the honor of being the earliest-known surviving Corvette.

Cozy Drive-In

The Cozy Drive-In in Netcong, New Jersey, serves up 1950s American roadside soul food to a devoted clientele of vintage car fans. A malted made of Good Humor ice cream, a towering Hamburger Royal, or a Texas Cheeseburger topped with the drive-in's own Texas Sauce all bring back fond memories of the glory days of roadside dining and classic cars. A 1957 Corvette convertible is parked in a berth while a 1963 Corvette Sting Ray coupe waits for a space. (Photograph © Lucinda Lewis/All Rights Reserved)

155

The Letter That Saved the Corvette

By Zora Arkus-Duntov

Zora Arkus-Duntov needs no introduction in these pages. The godfather of the Corvette is well known by all as the man who made the Corvette a success.

But things weren't always so. Soon after Zora joined Chevrolet's Corvette team, the fledgling car was slated to be canceled. Zora remembered walking down the hall in the General Motors building one day in 1954 only to be buttonholed by a higher-up in Chevrolet's sales department who was dressed in "uniform"—the then-fashionable outfit of a blue suit and yellow shoes. This salesman announced with glee, "The Corvette is finished—no more will be built!" It was an attitude endemic to the monolithic Chevrolet organization and its 6,000 dealerships, who were all geared to sell family cars in the millions. To these dealers and salesmen, the 1953 and 1954 Corvette was a misdirected flop.

Zora saw things differently. A fan of European sports cars and racing, he was also loyal to Chevrolet and firmly believed that the Corvette was key to the firm's future personality and long-term success. On October 15, 1954, Zora wrote the following memo to GM's Ed Cole and Maurice Olley urging them not to drop the Corvette and, instead, to boldly create a separate Corvette department within Chevrolet to oversee development.

Arkus-Duntov's famous memo has gone down in automotive legend as the Letter That Saved the Corvette although, at a company the size of Chevrolet, it surely took more than just one memo to change the tide. Nevertheless, in 1955, Arkus-Duntov was christened chief engineer in charge of the Corvette. The rest is history.

"Neon Classic"
A saved Corvette glistens in the neon glow of this painting by Scott Jacobs. (Artwork © 2002 by Scott Jacobs/Segal Fine Art)

TO	Mesars. E. N. Cole and M. Olley
ADDRESS	
FROM	Mr. Z. Arkus-Duntov
ADDRESS	Research & Development Section
SUBJECT	<u>CORVETTE</u>
DATE	October 15, 1954

In this note, I am speaking out of turn. I am giving options and suggestions without knowing all the factors. I realize this but still am offering my thoughts for what they are. In order to make the content clear and short, I will not use the polite apologetic phrasing and say, "it is" instead of "it possibly might be"—and I apologize for this now.

By the looks of it, the Corvette is on its way out.

I would like to say the following: Dropping the car now will have adverse effect internally and externally.

It is admission of failure. Failure of aggressive thinking in the eyes of the organization, failure to develop a salable product in the eyes of the outside world.

Above-said can be dismissed as sentimentality. Let's see if it can hurt the cash register. I think it can.

Ford enters the field with the Thunderbird, a car of the same class as the Corvette.

If Ford makes success where we failed, it may hurt.

With aggressiveness of Ford publicity, they may turn the fact to their advantage. I don't mean in terms of Thunderbird sales, but in terms of promotion of theirs and depreciation of our general lines.

We will leave an opening in which they can hit at will. "Ford out-engineered, outsold, or ran Chevrolet's pride and joy off the market". Maybe the idea is far-fetched. I can only gauge in terms of my own reactions or actions. In the bare-fisted fight we are in now, I would hit at any opening I could find and the situation where Ford enters and where Chevrolet retreats, it is not an opening, it is a hole!

Now if they can hurt us, then we can hurt them! We are one year ahead and we possibly learned some lessons which Ford has yet to learn.

Is the effort worthwhile? This, I am in no position to say. Obviously, in terms of direct sales a car for the discriminating low volume market is hardly an efficient investment of efforts. The value must be gauged by effects it may have on an overall picture.

The Corvette failed because it did not meet G.M. standards of a product. It did not have the value for the money.

If the value of a car consists of practical values and emotional appeal, the sports car has very little of the first and consequently has to have an exaggerated amount of the second. If a passenger car must have an appeal, nothing short of a mating call will extract $4,000 for a small two-seater. The Corvette as it was offered had curtailed practical value being a poor performer. With a 6-cylinder engine, it was no better than the medium priced family car.

Timing was also unfortunate. When the novelty appeal was the highest, we hadn't had the cars to sell. When the cars became available, hypnotized by the initial overwhelming response, no promotional effort was made.

The little promotion which was made was designed to depreciate the car rather than enhance it. Hundreds or possibly thousands of dollars contained in the price of a sports or luxury car are paid for exclusivity. What did our promotion say on the radio and advertised in magazines? "Now everybody can have it! Come and get it". What virtues did advertising extol? Only X inches high, only X inches long, etc. In the country, in which bigger is synonymous with better, and we really know it, we were trying to sell a car, because it is small! Crosley is smaller........

Were there no virtues to talk about? Quite some, but a condensation of best reports which appeared in motoring press previously had more glow and enthusiasm than our advertising.

Summarizing, the promotion was uninspired and half hearted attempt with no evidence of thought or enthusiasm.

Where do we stand now?

The Corvette still has the best and raciest look of all the sports cars, the Thunderbird included. Performance is far superior to all the passenger cars and to 99% of the sports cars used on the road. It has flow in respect to passenger protection. Water leaks and cumbersome top and side window. With these minor flaws removed, we have a sports car with as much practical value as the sports car can have.

Survivor

The Corvette survived to be revived in 1955, thanks in large part to Zora Arkus-Duntov's farsighted vision. The sports car now had the V-8 power it needed to battle Ford's Thunderbird. This 1955 Gypsy Red convertible was one of just 700 Corvettes built this year, the second-lowest production year following the car's 1953 debut. (Photograph © Jerry Heasley)

The borderline between the value and lack of same is not the absolute performance but comparative one. "My car can go X miles per hour does not mean as much as "My car can trim anything on wheels". The '55 Corvette will have this pride attached to its ownership. To be a success, it will need more emotional appeal which can be provided by promotion which will fit the product and inflame the type of customers which can buy the car.

As I see it and put it down, the Corvette is a product different from a passenger automobile having in every phase of operation problems of its own. With sales potential between 3 and at the most 10,000 cars a year, it is bound to be a hindering step-child in an organization which acts and thinks in terms of 1,500,000 units. A subdivision, section, department or what not, but an organization no matter how small but which is directly responsible for the successes of operation is necessary.

An organization which will eat and sleep Corvette as our divisions are eating and sleeping their particular cars.

I am convinced that a group with concentrated objective will not only stand a chance to achieve the desired result, but devise ways and means to make the operation profitable in a direct business sense.

Z. Arkus-Duntov

ZAD:he